The Annotated

NORTHWEST PASSAGE

The Annotated
NORTHWEST PASSAGE

by

Scott Chantler

Book Design by

Keith Wood

Collection Edited by

Randal C. Jarrell with *Jill Beaton*

Original Series Edited by

Randal C. Jarrell and *James Lucas Jones*

Published by Oni Press, Inc.

Joe Nozemack, publisher
James Lucas Jones, editor in chief
Randal C. Jarrell, managing editor
Doug Sherwood, editorial assistant
Jill Beaton, editorial intern

ONI PRESS, INC.
1305 SE Martin Luther King Jr. Blvd.
Suite A
Portland, OR 97214
USA

www.onipress.com
www.scottchantler.com

First edition: June 2007
ISBN-13: 978-1-932664-61-4
ISBN-10: 1-932664-61-0

1 3 5 7 9 10 8 6 4 2

Printed In Singapore.

The Annotated

NORTHWEST PASSAGE

Prologue

Rupert's Land,
1755.

I am *Eagle Eye*, of the Cree.

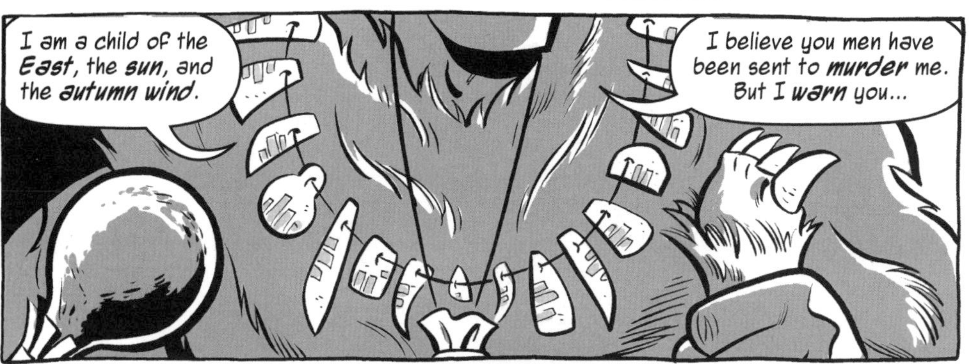
I am a child of the *East*, the *sun*, and the *autumn wind*.
I believe you men have been sent to *murder* me. But I *warn* you...

...I have killed a great number of White men, and will kill you, too, if even one of you steps closer.

I aim to go to the trading post below. Anyone trying to stop me who does not die will have to face the justice of the English.
They do not take kindly to the massacre of Red men in these parts.

Worse, he will have the curse of my people upon him.

CLICK!

So be it.

The Annotated

NORTHWEST PASSAGE

Chapter 1

"Arrivals and Departures"

HBC
Gentlemen!
Thank you, one and all, for joining me this evening.

As you all know, I'll soon be stepping down as the Company's overseas governor...

...And that the next supply ship brings with it your **new** governor, Sir Walter Hargrove.

Hargrove is an old Navy man, and he's going to be ***tough*** on this lot.

He's going to expect you to ***work hard***...
BOO!
...Keep yourselves neat in appearance...
BOO!
...And most of all, turn a profit for the Company.

I have no doubt that he'll find the occupants of Fort Newcastle equal to the task.
You men are uniquely suited for life here in Rupert's Land--hardy, intelligent, self-reliant.

Survivors.

I'm going to miss all of these faces...

...Except for *yours*, Hob.
HAHAHAH
Huh-huh. Thank yuh, Guv'ner.

If you give Hargrove the same level of devoted service that I've enjoyed these past ten years, he'll have no problem turning this into the kind of operation one would expect from the largest trading post on Hudson's Bay!

I almost wish I were going to be here to see it.

Though I'll be taking the ship back to England when it departs, my son Simon will remain, here in the land of his birth.
And my sister's youngest son, who has recently signed up with the Company--against his father's wishes, I might add--has been assigned here as a clerk, and will arrive alongside Governor Hargrove.
In other words, any of you men get out of line, and I'll ***hear*** about it.

As some of you may have heard, a band of Chippewa who came to trade reported seeing an English ship sailing into the Bay about three weeks ago.
That means it could be here as early as tomorrow, my friends, with new men and fresh provisions...

...So tonight let's empty the kegs!
It's my *retirement* party!

HURRAY FOR GOVERNOR LORD! HURR OR GOVERNOR LORD!
Nice speech, sir.

You know, Duncan, you *used* to call me "Charles"...not to mention things a whole lot worse.
That was before you were the governor, sir.

So when Hargrove relieves me, we can go back to the old days when we were just friends, rather than master and slave?
Love to...

...Sir.

So, Charles, looking forward to finally going home?
Home?
Reverend, I've not seen England in over twenty years. Nearly half my lifetime.

I'm not sure I'll even recognise it.

Oh, come now...it may take some getting used to after living all these years in the wild, but think of the comforts you'll be able to enjoy which you've been denied out here for so long!

I've had far *too many* comforts the last decade or so.
I'm not built for huddling in a fort, counting pelts.

Ah, but just imagine yourself in a cosy sitting room, with a glass of sherry that doesn't have to be rationed, warming by a fire, writing your memoirs...
Writing my *what?*

Now Charles, surely you intend to write about your adventures in the New World! In your day, you were one of the greatest explorers since *Radisson* and *Des Groseilliers!*

In my day?!
Let me tell you something. I--

Governor?

I think you should probably see this.

How is he, Reverend?
He's going to *live*, if that's what you mean.

I expect he will.
He always has.

You **know** this man?

We ***both*** do.
He's one of our men, from the old days. A Cree shaman by the name of ***Eagle Eye***.
But neither of us had seen him in ***years!***

A ***shaman?*** Not a Christian?
He keeps his ***own*** counsel on matters of faith...
...As we ***all*** should.

I always assumed your tolerance of heathen superstition was simply for the sake of ***diplomacy***.
I've ***seen*** the Red Man's magic at work, Reverend...

...It may not be as much hokum as you ***think***.

You there!
Lend a hand, would you?

Oh.
Young Master Lord.
My apologies. I didn't know it was you.

You men are working late.

Well, no one felt much like celebratin' after yer father left the party.
'Sides, there's lots to be done, gettin' the *Furs* ready to be loaded and whatnot.

Yes...
...We wouldn't want the people of England to wait a moment more than they *had* to for their ridiculous *Furry hats*.

You men break your backs all you want for such lunacy. I'm certain that the *accountants* are already sleeping well, atop *large piles of money* made from your toil.

Very well, then.
Sorry to *disturb* you.

Come on, men! Let's move those barrels...

...There's a *fog* movin' in!

What d'you suppose he was doing out there all alone?
D'you think he was comin' **here?** Stoppin' in to say 'ello after all these years?

And who on Earth would have **attacked** him?
I can't imagine it was any of his **own** people, given his station. And I refuse to believe that it was any of **ours**.

Blackfoot, maybe?
This far east?
I don't know, Duncan...if the Blackfoot came to the Bay, surely they'd be coming to **trade**, not start a war with the Cree.

It's damn peculiar, however you look at it.
You sure you want to retire, and miss all this excitement?

What?
What is it?
What's what?

All you've done fer months is scowl at the thought of returning to England, now suddenly you look like the cat's uncle Gringog.
Somethin' you wanna tell me?

Now that the time is almost here, old friend, I'm going to let you in on a *little secret*...
...I am not *truly* retiring.

There's a new governor on that ship out there who thinks *differently*, I'm afraid.
Oh, I'm retiring as the governor of Fort Newcastle, that's for certain. I've had more than enough of life as a *businessman*.

If the Company still put any stock in *exploration*, that'd be one thing.
But they *don't*, Duncan. Not anymore.

When you and I were young, there was still some interest in seeing what was around the next corner.
And joining the Company was an opportunity to find out.

You and I, John Blackmoon, Barclay, Watt, Quick Jack, old Eagle Eye in there...we'd strike out with crude maps and a couple of heavily laden canoes, and see what there was to see.
One step ahead of the French, ahead of Montglave and his men.
It wasn't just for ourselves, or the Company, but for ***King and country***.

But for years now the Company has been content to sit here on the Bay, hunkered in forts, making the Indians come to *us* to trade.
And all the while the French continue to push inland.

When I return to England, I intend to take this argument up with the shareholders, and, if need be, the King himself.

I'll convince them to give me a *ship*, maybe a few, and...

This is about the *Passage*, isn't it?
Your fabled *Northwest Passage!*

Dear *God*, sir!
You and I know the land from here to the mountains as well as anyone, save the Indians.
If there's a route to China by sea it isn't to the west of here, nor the north, and *certainly* not to the south.

It's high time you--and every *other* explorer since Columbus--stopped chasing that old dream.
It's not *there*, sir. It doesn't *exist*.

But what's *beyond* those mountains, Duncan? The edge of the world? A steep drop off into *Oblivion?*
Or perhaps--just *perhaps*--an *ocean*.
The *Pacific*.
The mountains have to drain *somewhere* on that side, after all.

The Passage **exists**, my friend. And I'm going to **find** it.
In a **frigate** or in a **canoe**, I'm going to find it.
All I need to do is get the hell out of this **fort**, once and for all.

Of course, I'll have need of a **steersman**...
OH NO!
Stop **right there!**

I've **done** my bit, sir, and unlike yerself, I'm lookin' forward to puttin' in another few years and then settlin' down someplace comfy, like Reverend Kirby says.
Maybe out in Nova Scotia, or down New England way.

No more adventures fer **me**, thank you very much!

HAMLET
Prince of Denmark
by
William Shakespeare
What you readin', Mr. Fletcher?

Hmm? Oh, it's *Hamlet*.
Huh.

What's it about?

"What's it *about?*"
My dear Warwick, are you telling me that you've never experienced the deep pleasures of Shakespeare's masterpiece?
Never 'eard of 'im.

"Never HEARD of him?!"
Shakespeare! The great English dramatist and poet! The Bard of Avon!
Dear *God*, man, he's the yardstick against which society measures its literacy!

Is 'e now?
That ain't so impressive. McPhee over here is the yardstick against which society measures ***whisky consumption***.
You ever 'eard of this Shakespeare fella, McPhee?
⟨Burp!⟩
In't he the one-eyed feller 'oo married yer cousin?

There y'are, Mr. Fletcher, two 'gainst one.
Hrmph.

Mr. Fletcher...!

"...Governor Hargrove is asking for you on deck."
Not much wind tonight...seems like we're barely moving.
Yes, sir.

It'll pick up in the morning, I suspect.
I hope you're right, Governor.

Beg your pardon, Master Hargrove...

Templeton Fletcher!
Walk with me a while, would you?

I used to like to stroll the deck of my ***own*** ship at night. Nothing better for clearing the mind, and invigorating the body.
I just wish this damned fog would lift so we could see something of the countryside.
With any luck the wind will start blowing again and we'll sail clear of it.
Is there something you wished to speak with me about, Governor?

There ***is***, in fact. I've just heard a rumour among the crew that you're the nephew of Charles Lord. Is this ***true?***
It is indeed, sir.

Fascinating man, your uncle, as I understand it.
You would know as well as I, actually. I've never met him. He's been in Rupert's Land with the Company since before I was born.
Though I've read ***most***, if not ***all***, of what's been written of his adventures.

And my **mother** speaks highly of him, of course.
Just your mother? Not your father?

My father is a...**different** sort of creature than Charles Lord, if you take my meaning, sir.
I think I do.
Your father is a **merchant?**

A shareholder in the Company, in fact.
The type of man who's content to venture nothing but **capital**, and get fat and rich off the backs of men like my uncle.
I **see**.

Let me make **another** guess, if I may, son.
You signed on with the Company, and accepted a post in the most God-forsaken part of the Empire, as a way of proving that you're a man like your **uncle**, and not a man like your **father**.

Because you're worried that it might be the other way around.

Is it ***that*** obvious?
Ha!
Indeed it ***is***, my boy.

Do I really need to tell you how much you stand out from the rest of the men?
An ***Oxford dandy*** among the saltiest of Welshmen and Orcadians?
SCRITCH!

Is this truly what you'd envisioned for yourself, lad?
Nine months a year of cold that'd kill a man in minutes, followed by three of enough mosquitoes and blackflies to drive him ***mad?***
Working until you feel like you're going to ***keel over***, then working some ***more?***

Will that much physical labour be required of a ***clerk***, sir?
It will if I ***say*** so.
There'll be no room for anyone unable to pull their weight--and the weight of the man ***next*** to him, if necessary.

If you thought you were going to sit in the counting room and be rewarded with a quick promotion, you thought wrong.

If you thought you were going to find a life of adventure and make a name for yourself, you thought wrong again. It's not like it was in your uncle's day.
Outpost life isn't exciting, or even the least bit interesting, and he'd be the first to tell you so.

These other men aren't here on some romantic personal quest, lad.
They're hard workers, and the best they can hope for is to spend a handful of difficult years in Rupert's Land, then return with enough in their pockets to take a wife and set themselves up in a life that's comfortable, and not much more.

I know you've had some difficulty adjusting to the men. They must seem like hopeless dullards to you.
As an educated man myself, I can sympathize.

But believe me, as soon as we go ashore, you'll be the one trying to catch up. This is a beautiful land, but a harsh one. All the books in England aren't going to help you where we're going.

So ***please***, go a little easier on them. There's a lot these men can teach you that you won't learn from Milton or Chaucer.
After all, if I read you correctly, I believe that's why you're here.
Yes, sir. ***Thank*** you, sir.

Good.
Now, why don't you go back below and get some rest...

We'll likely be putting in tomorrow, and it's going to busy, bus--

What on ***Earth***...?
What ***is*** it, sir?

I have no idea.
But I think you'd better rouse the captain.

The Annotated

NORTHWEST PASSAGE

Chapter 2

"Fire and Water"

How's the weather out there this morning?
Hmm?

The weather.
Smooth sailing, do you suppose?
Oh. The supply ship.
I think they'll be making headway, yes.
Me, too. I think they'll be here today.
I've got a feeling.

Simon.
Son.
I--
Excuse me, sir...
...Reverend Kirby to see you.

Reverend!
Have you eaten? Please, join us...
That's quite all right, Charles, thank you...sorry to interrupt your breakfast.

I wanted to be the first to tell you that the lookouts have spotted a *sail* on the horizon. Officers and men alike are gathering down at the shore.

Splendid!
Any news of our *visitor?* He's still alive, I dare hope?

He's alive, all right. And *awake.*
And asking for *you.*

Then you are the bearer of much good news, indeed!
Excuse us, Simon...

...But before I get on that ship, I have one last piece of business to attend to.

Eagle Eye,
you old devil!

You've looked better.
As have you, old friend.
Rich White man's clothes look as uncomfortable on you as they would on **me**.

Charles is the local governor now. It's been a while since he's worn **buckskin**.

I can **tell**.

But it makes me glad to see you alive, Charles.
I might say the same to ***you***.

It will take more than your Christian medicine to kill ***me***, old friend.

Well, I nev--
Now, now...don't let the robe and collar fool you. Kirby here is more than our resident chaplain. He's also a ***fine*** surgeon.

It's my understanding that he pulled enough musket balls out of you for a St. George's Day shooting match.
You owe him your ***life***, there's no two ways about it.

You are right. I mean no offence.
The Great Spirit and your Christian God are one in the same. It is only we men who think them different.

Fair enough.
Now why don't you tell me what happened? Who did this to you? And what brings you back here, after all these years?

It is a long tale, Charles, and not a happy one.
I did not joke when I said I was glad to see you alive. It means that I am not too late.
You see, I have come to ***warn*** you.

To warn you of your own ***death.***

Bring them aboard, men!
MAID MARIAN

Gently, now! They're your fellow countrymen, by the look of them!

This one is an officer.
Make sure he gets a proper bed, will you, Garson?

What do you suppose happened to them?
Survivors of a sinking, perhaps. Or a mutiny.

Whoever they are, they must have been days off course. There wasn't even supposed to *be* another English vessel in the Bay.

What will happen to them now?
Some will die, no doubt. Depends on how long they'd been out there.
The ones who live will be absorbed into the crew until the ship gets back to England.

We'll make room for them as best we can, lad...

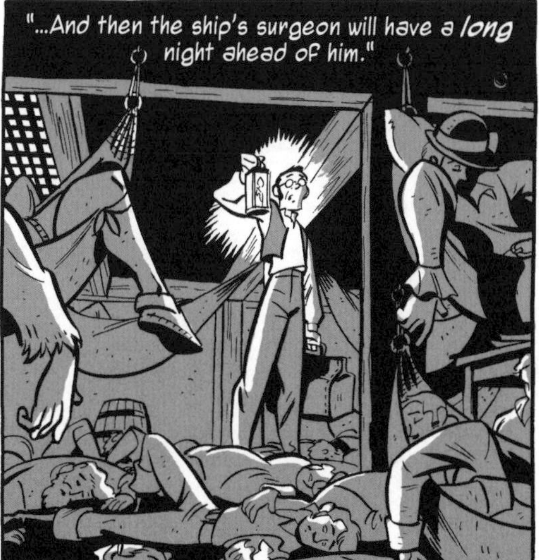
"...And then the ship's surgeon will have a *long* night ahead of him."

You had a *vision?*
One of the strongest I have *ever* had.

Tell me.
From the beginning.

In the years since we last saw each other, I have wandered far, from village to village, healing and using my gifts however they can be of the most help.

"In one small village, I met a girl named Nacoma.
"She was with child, and asked me what was in the future for her baby.
"I told her I would ask the Great Spirit. So I climbed to a high place and fasted...
"...For four days...
"...And four nights...

"Then the *Eagle*
came to me.

"I asked the Eagle of the child of Nacoma and Kawacatoose.
"It told me there would be no such child. That Nacoma was *dead.*
"I asked how that could be, and the Eagle showed me.
"It was a vision I will not soon forget.

"When the Eagle finally let me go, I climbed back down to the village.

"I knew what I would find, but that did not make it ***easier***."

The whole village, *destroyed?* My *God!* Were there no--
Survivors?
The few, if any, must have fled into the forest. But there were a lot of dead, my friend.

"A *lot* of dead."

Who did it? Blackfoot?
If it had been the Blackfoot, Charles, it would not have been necessary to warn *you.*

This was not tribe against tribe. These killers were well-armed. Clumsy in their tactics.
White.

* "I swear the blood will never come off. How many do you think we killed?"

French troops in Cree territory?

Not exactly.

"They were not military. They wore no uniforms.

"They were unorganized. Undisciplined. A ***rabble.***"

Rogue traders, perhaps?

They were too many in number for that. And why murder your customers?

Mercenaries, then.

But mercenaries working for ***whom?***

That I could not tell. But I learned one more thing as I listened to their chatter...

Crois-tu que nous trouverons un jour ce chaman?*
Qui sait? Je trouve qu'ils se ressemblent tous...**
* "Do you think we'll ever find this shaman?"
** "Who knows? They all look the same to me..."
"That they were tracking a wandering shaman who they had followed to that village.
"They had been sent to kill ***me.***
"I tried to slip away unnoticed, hoping to make it here to Fort Newcastle without them following me.
"Normally, it would be easy. A Red man who does not want to be seen by White eyes usually is ***not*** seen.
"But it did not take long for them to miss one of their ***canoes.***
Voleur!

"They chased me most of the way up river.
"Eventually, I took to the land, thinking my chances of out-running them better in the forest.
"But they were already too close.
"I was within sight of the fort when they finally caught me.
"I am not the warrior I once was, Charles. And I was too busy fighting to call any of the Grandfathers to my aid.
CRAK!
"I buried my knife in one of them...
"...And another will not have use of his right arm again.
POOM!
"But after that...
POOM!
POOM!

"They knew I was the shaman they had been sent to kill. And they thought they had finally done it.
"Even *I* thought they had.
"But they were worried about being seen, and had no time to make sure."

Well, thank God--or the Great Spirit, if you prefer--that my hunters found you when they did.
You're safe now. I don't know why these men were after you, or who sent them, but it'll take more than a handful of untrained irregulars to get in ***here***.

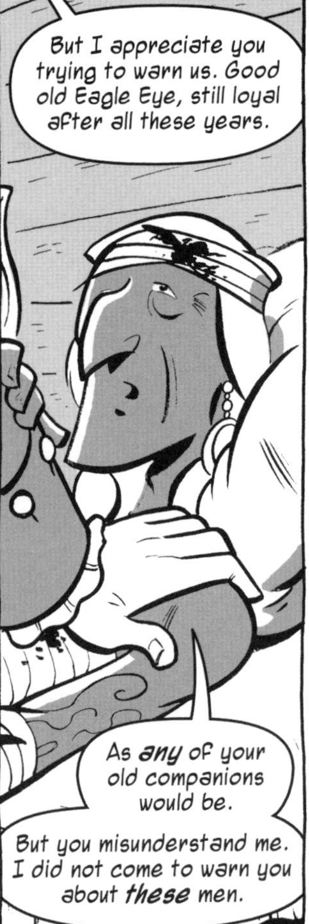
But I appreciate you trying to warn us. Good old Eagle Eye, still loyal after all these years.
As ***any*** of your old companions would be.
But you misunderstand me. I did not come to warn you about ***these*** men.

These men, whoever they were, somehow knew that I would be the only one who might see the ***greater threat***, and warn you against it.
Greater than killing Cree women and children? Eagle Eye--

Your surgeon tells me that a supply ship is coming, to carry you back to Europe.
I urge you not to get on it.
This has to do with the rest of your vision.
Yes.
"The Eagle wanted to show me more.
"He showed me the Bay.
"It was full of bodies. **English** bodies.
"And one of them had **your** face."

The French wouldn't dare attack the supply ship. It would be considered an act of **war!**
Then war it will be.
It is a ship of death, old friend. All aboard it will be ***doomed***.

Are you sure it was ***me*** that you saw?
That is why you must warn Simon as well. The Grandfathers can be cryptic in how they reveal the future. It may be you...

...or one of your ***kin***.

Dear God.

The SHIP!
MAID M

On a eu de la chance qu'ils nous aient vus dans le brouillard...*
* "We were lucky they saw us in the fog..."

Ils n'ont rien vu venir...*
* "They had no idea what was coming..."

...Ces Anglais sont beaucoup trop confiants!*
* "...These Englishmen are far too trusting!"

Avons-nous réussi? Est-ce que tous les Anglais sont morts?*

* "Have we done it? Are the English all dead?"

But, I can sympathise with you. I abhor violence, myself--though this is not a malady that is shared by my men, obviously, especially *Zev* here.
While some of your fellows might have thought you a coward, their thoughts are inconsequential, as they are all dead, and you, clearly, are still alive.

Though for how *long* remains to be seen.
Please, sir, don't kill me. M-my father is a wealthy man, he will--

How wealthy?

Very wealthy, sir. If you spare me, he will reward you handsomely. You have my solemn word!
The word of an English coward means not'ing to Guerin Montglave!

That you could have become a respected leader in New France, but chose instead to become a privateer, allying yourself with mercenaries and rogue traders, forcing increasingly hostile encounters with the English.

Ah.
Lord.
I suppose you English fancy him some sort of ***folk hero***, no? A fur trader with no religion, who fathered a bastard son on a filthy, how do you say, ***"bit of brown"***?

I have decided your fate, Englishman.
You will ***live***, for now.
I want one of you alive. To bear witness to what is going to happen next.

You see, in the morning, I will seize control of the fur trade in Hudson's Bay.
In the process, Charles Lord will ***die***.

We shall see then what your false English legends are made of.

The Annotated

NORTHWEST PASSAGE

Chapter 3

"John and Jack"

How much **Further**, Mister Reaney?

For the last time, Ross, I don't bloody *know!*
When exactly do you suppose I had time to outfit myself with a *map?*
I--
SNAP!
OWWW!
Dammit, men...I've twisted my ankle.
Somebody give me a hand up.

As the only OFFICER among you, I'm ORDERING one of you to give me a hand up!

Thank you, MacDougal.
I'm beginning to see now why our Governor counts you the best among the men.

I swear that sometimes he seems to value you more than even some of the officers.
I can't imagine.

I think, too, that I owe you an apology for not heeding your advice about following the shore.
It's all right. As long as the Bay is to our right, we'll know we're headin' north.

Is it still to our right?
It is.
Very good, then.

You might want to ease up a wee bit on the men, sir, if you don't mind my sayin'.
I know that you were postmaster an' all, but our Company ranks don't mean fiddlesticks out here.

Some of these men have been traipsin' through the forests here since you were hidin' under yer mother's skirt.
All due respect, of course.
Of course.
Anything *else* I should know?

Just that we're being *followed*.
What?
For how long?

At least two days. Maybe three.
And you didn't say anything until *now?*

I wanted to be sure. Whoever it is, they're good. Practically *invisible-like*.
But they're there.

If it's ***them***, wanting to finish the job, why don't they just get it over with?
I don't think it's any of Montglave's men.

Reds, then?
Maybe. But I don't think so.
Keep it under yer hat fer now, until I find out exactly what we're dealin' with...

SNAP!

Jeb?

Jeb?!

JE--!

SHIK!

Hello, John.
Good to see you again.

So what brings *you* out of hidin' after all these years? I thought you'd sworn off contact with Whites.

I've been tracking a small army that's been on the move through these parts.
I first picked up their scent south of James Bay... I think they came overland from New France.

And you thought we were them.
They broke into two groups along the way. I followed one until they took to the water. I thought you might be the other.

I spotted you once or twice, but none of the others did.
You haven't lost your touch. You're still the best tracker in Rupert's Land.

If I were *blind* I could track the man leading you.
Where is Charles?
Well now, that's gonna require some explainin'.

The "small army" you've been followin' captured Fort Newcastle a little more than five days ago.
Except fer Charles, what you see here are all that remains of its inhabitants.

"The supply ship had been captured. No one on shore knew it, of course, so it just sailed right up, Union Jack wavin'...

"...Then turned broadside and began firin'."

"When I say nobody knew,
I mean beside ***Charles***.
"He came out of the blue, lookin' like God's revenge against murder, yellin' fer folks to get back inside the walls.
"We found out later that Eagle Eye had warned him. He'd seen somethin' in one of his visions.
"It was too little, too late, though.
"A lot of 'em never knew what hit 'em.
"We still don't know ***what*** happened to Eagle Eye.
"Our ***own*** cannons were unmanned.
"After all, why defend yerself from yer own bloody supply ship?

"Them who could still stand started runnin' back to the fort.
"But then, out of the trees, comes a ***second*** attack.
"It was a ***bloodbath***, John, I'm here to tell ya.
"A handful of us made it, and were preparin' to make a stand, tryin' to find anythin' to use as a weapon.

"That's when
we saw him.
"We caught a glimpse
of the man who was
attackin' us.
"Who was
beatin'
us.
"It was *Guerin
Montglave*."

"So we made for the trees, what few of us were left.

"We had to ***drag*** Charles, who kept screaming for his son."

SIMON!!!

We don't know what happened to Simon, either. If he stayed at the fort, I fear the worst.
That boy's always been the wilful sort, and if the bunch of us said retreat, it'd be just like him to do anythin' *but*.
I remember.
So what *now?*

We need shelter, and medical help for some of these men. So we're headed to Fort Duchess of York.
Hopefully they've enough supplies left that they can take us in. Though they won't be happy about the extra rationin'.

Then what?

When the *Maid Marian* doesn't return to Gravesend, the King'll send out a man-o-war. Maybe two.
Things are a bit chalky with France right now. More than usual, even. He won't think she just sank.

A couple of ships, and some marines...we'll have the fort back by this time next year.

Damn, John, it really *is* good to see you. In a fight, you're worth any ten other men.
There's no one I'd rather have at our side when it finally comes down between Charles and that canker-blossom Montglave. You couldn't have come back at a better time.

I'm not a Company employee anymore, Duncan. I haven't been for a long time.
What makes you think I care anything for the wars between English and French?

Because you were an Englishman, once.
And even if you weren't, this is for a friend. It's for **Charles**.

He went inland, didn't he? Looking for Jack Prince.
If we can find Quick Jack and his men, the fort'll be ours again before the first snowfall.
Sooner, if *you're* with us, too.

He won't come.
He hates the Company. And he hates Charles.
Not as much as he hates Montglave.

I wouldn't count on it.

How about Watt, and Barclay?
Watt went back to England in '48. He's a tailor, if you can believe it.
And Barclay's war-caperin' days were short-lived. He was hanged in New France after a failed attempt to capture Louisbourg.

I'll help any way I can, old friend.
Because you need it more than you think.

I tell you, Jack'll help if Charles can find h--
I don't mean *that*.
The trail I'd been following--Montglave's trail--*ended* at Fort Duchess of York.

You aren't going to like what you find there.

Visit, Lord, we pray, this place...
KRASHHH!

PLEASE! Don't shoot!

You are t'e fort surgeon, non?
Also its chaplain.

I would not shoot a man of t'e cloth.
B'sides, we will need you to treat some of our *blessé*--our *wounded*. Our own doctor did not last two weeks outside of civilization.
Thank you. Thank you.

Any patients in t'ere?
Just one.

Please! He's barely alive as it is...!
No one in 'ere, Reverend.
Are you *lyin'* to us, Englishman?
No.
No, I *swear*...
...He was here a moment ago.

BAM!

Where is he?

POOM!

Where is Charles Lord?!

He isn't here.

You should have fled when you had the chance, Englishman!
Show yourself!

Hold your fire,
messieurs.

You are the
half-breed son,
are you not?

Lord's
boy by his
"*country*
wife."
I have heard of
you, of course. But
never imagined I would
lay eyes on you.

Now, where *is* he, garcon? I will ask only once.
I told you. He isn't here.
I saw him run for the trees with some of the others.

I *like* this one.
We will spare him, for now.

Monsieur Montglave!
Le combat est fini. Le fort est à nous.*
* "The fighting is over. The fort is ours."

Et nous avons quelques *prisonniers*...*
* "And we have some *prisoners*..."

Gunpowder? Three pounds?
Two made-beaver.

Mistahi!
It's a fair trade, take it or leave it.
Kwaskwipicikan...

Kwaskwipicikan! Nisotanaw!
Where's Speck?

He wants twenty fishhooks.

Two made-beaver. *Niso.*
Peyak! Peyak!

One?!
Listen, the bloody Hudson's Bay Company would want ***three***!
Two made-beaver, no less.

Mahti kawioa kayiyisihitotan...
He thinks you're cheating him.

He says he could get a better trade from...from the "other White man".
Well, he's welcome to try. It's ***three weeks*** to the Bay from here.

Jack, I think this is going to get ugly...

Everybody just **stay calm**.
We'll head back to the canoe, nice and slow-like. Big smiles. We're all friends here...

No reason for things to get out of h--
OWW!

Well, folks, I was enjoyin' the party just fine, right up until y'all started gettin' a little **shove-y**.
click!
click!

Now I suggest you get back into your tepees, or your wigwams, or whatever the hell you call 'em...
...Because any man takes another step, or jabs one of those pig-stickers at me, is going to wake up tomorrow missing his *goddamn* **HEAD!**

Tell 'em, Speck.

Ponihta mahti! *Stop!*

Well, I'll be damned...

I can't believe it.
This was the most heavily fortified post in North America. I thought she'd **never** fall!
How'd he **do** it, John?
He knows the land, and knows his enemy.

He'd have known, for instance, that
the cannons here all face the water.
So he came from the landside.

But the ***walls!*** These're ***stone,*** fer Christ's sake!
They can still be scaled. At night, or the break of dawn. The watchman asleep, or looking the other way.

They dropped grenades into the buildings. Smoked them out.
Then shot them as they ran from the flames.

Some boats are missing.
Their trail ends here. They took to the sea...

...Then captured the supply ship, usin' it 'gainst Fort Newcastle.
I hate that mangy cur Montglave. But I have to admit he pulled one over on all of us.

He doesn't fight like a European.
He strikes quickly, and without warning. Uses trickery, and deception.

He aims to put his enemy down as quickly as possible, and make sure they don't get up again.

Indian style.

Any survivors, d'you think?
If there were, I suspect you'd have encountered them on the way.
They'd have been heading for Fort Newcastle, same as you were coming here.

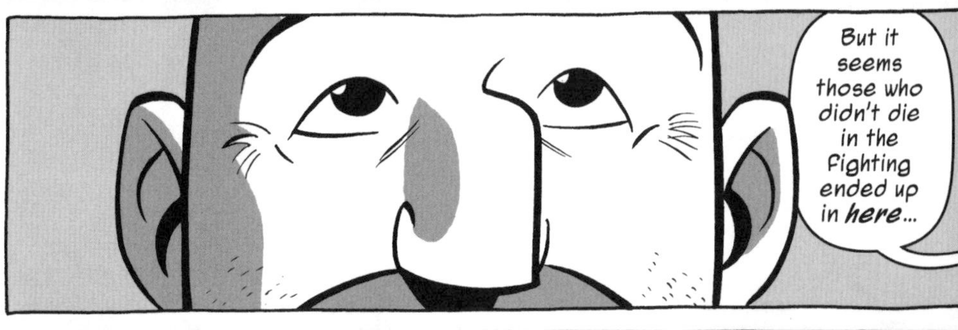
But it seems those who didn't die in the fighting ended up in ***here***...

Non.

Not t'is.
Not again.
You said, m'sieur, t'at t'ere would be no more executions.

Just what did you think you signed up for, René de Cuthbert? A parade? You are guns for hire, are you not?
You 'ired us to capture some English forts, and we 'ave done it.

But now you 'ave men razing an Indian village, and Amaury and I cannot for the life of us figure out what t'e Indians 'ave got to do wit' any of t'is.
If anyt'ing, you should be using t'em to fight 'gainst the English!

Too much blood 'as been spilled, m'sieur. We were willing to do it, for t'e money.
But t'is...t'is is *cruel*. It is *torture*.

Zev?

POOM!

How did you know we'd even *be* here?
I didn't.
Given the time of year, though, I knew you'd be heading back east, and knew you'd surely be stopping at every Cree camp along the way.
When I got here and they told me you hadn't yet passed by, I waited until you did.
So how long have you *been* here?
Nearly a week. But I'd have spent longer than that searching for you on the river, and may have missed you entirely.

And you came all this way because you think I'm going to help you get Fort Newcastle back?
You're the best man I've ever seen with a pistol and sword, Jack. We need you.

And if you can convince your men, then we'll finally send Montglave to the Hell where he belongs.
There'll be a job with the Company for each of them, if we succeed.

My men?
Charles, my men don't care **who** you are, and they **hate** the Company.
Hell, you're our **competition!**

Competition or no, you know as well as I do that whoever controls the Bay controls the fur trade.
Right now, **Montglave** controls it. Is that what you want?

Wouldn't be my first choice.
But having French forts on the Bay ***is*** rather attractive. It'd save us the trip back to Montreal.

WHAT?!
You'd deal with that rusty-gutted son of a bitch?
Maybe.

He probably wouldn't deal with **me**. He'd probably have me killed on sight, just like he would you. I don't know. Montglave may be a villain...
...But he never did anything to me like what **you** did.

How can you--?!

Jack, listen. That was **years** ago. And I was **hoping** that you'd have grown up enough to realise there are **rules** which--

You and your damned **rules!**
Any **rule** that says you take the lash to your friends isn't **worth** following!

Listen, I--
Discipline is ***important*** out here. We're thousands of miles from the nearest court, you know that...
Would you prefer if one of the ***other*** officers administer the punishment, sir?
No.
"Everyone knew that you were trading behind our backs. How could I ever have kept order without punishing you?"
I'll do it ***myself***.

With a *whip*, Charles?!
Why not a *fine?* Why not short my rations, or throw me in *jail?*

You whipped me, like a damn *slave!*
Would you have done that to Watt? To John?

To *Duncan?*

Jack...

Anyone *else* have complaints about the working conditions?

What about *you*, de Cuthbert?

Without *discipline*, mes amis...

...How can we have *order?*

In the name of all that's holy, you aren't ***actually*** going to hang these men, are you?
I would not even ***think*** of it, Reverend.

You are.
You and your young friend here.

Do I need to explain what happens if you ***refuse?***

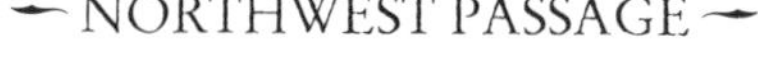

You were like a son to me, Jack. You and John both.
If I'd done any less, it would have looked like I was going easy on you because of it.

If I'd known you would desert, I would have done things differently.
You've been missed, more than you know.

I'm **sorry,** Jack. I truly am.

I'd have been gone sooner or later, old man. I couldn't take one more year cooped up.
I can't believe that *you* lasted so long. And now you want to go *back!*

Do whatever you need to. Me, I've got a season's worth of pelts to haul back to New France. And it's late enough in the season as it is.

Now you *could* go running back there, telling yourself that it's for King and country and to rescue any survivors.
But we both know that Simon is as dead as this nephew of yours, and that it'd *really* be so that you and Montglave can kill each other for old times' sake.

But I'm guessing that this time you've spent in the backcountry is already beginning to remind you how much you loved this life.
I can't go with you, Charles...

...But why don't *you* come with *us*?

What?

You still look strong as an ox, and we could use you. Charles Lord and Quick Jack, just like the old days.
We could even be *partners*, if you want.

We've been going *deep*, old man. Deeper every season.
Into the prairies. Further, even. And north as far as Athabasca.

Hell, I wouldn't be surprised if we stumble upon the *Northwest Passage* one of these days.

What do you say?

The Annotated

NORTHWEST PASSAGE

Chapter 4

"Freedom and Captivity"

The nights are getting colder.

What will we do when winter comes? It's hard enough *inside*.
We'll adapt. Or we'll die.

Well, *that's* comforting.
And what if this Guerin Montglave and his men come looking for us? We're in no shape to fight...

I've sent John Blackmoon to patrol between here and Fort Newcastle. No one will get past *him*.
ONE MAN?!
What if they *kill* him?

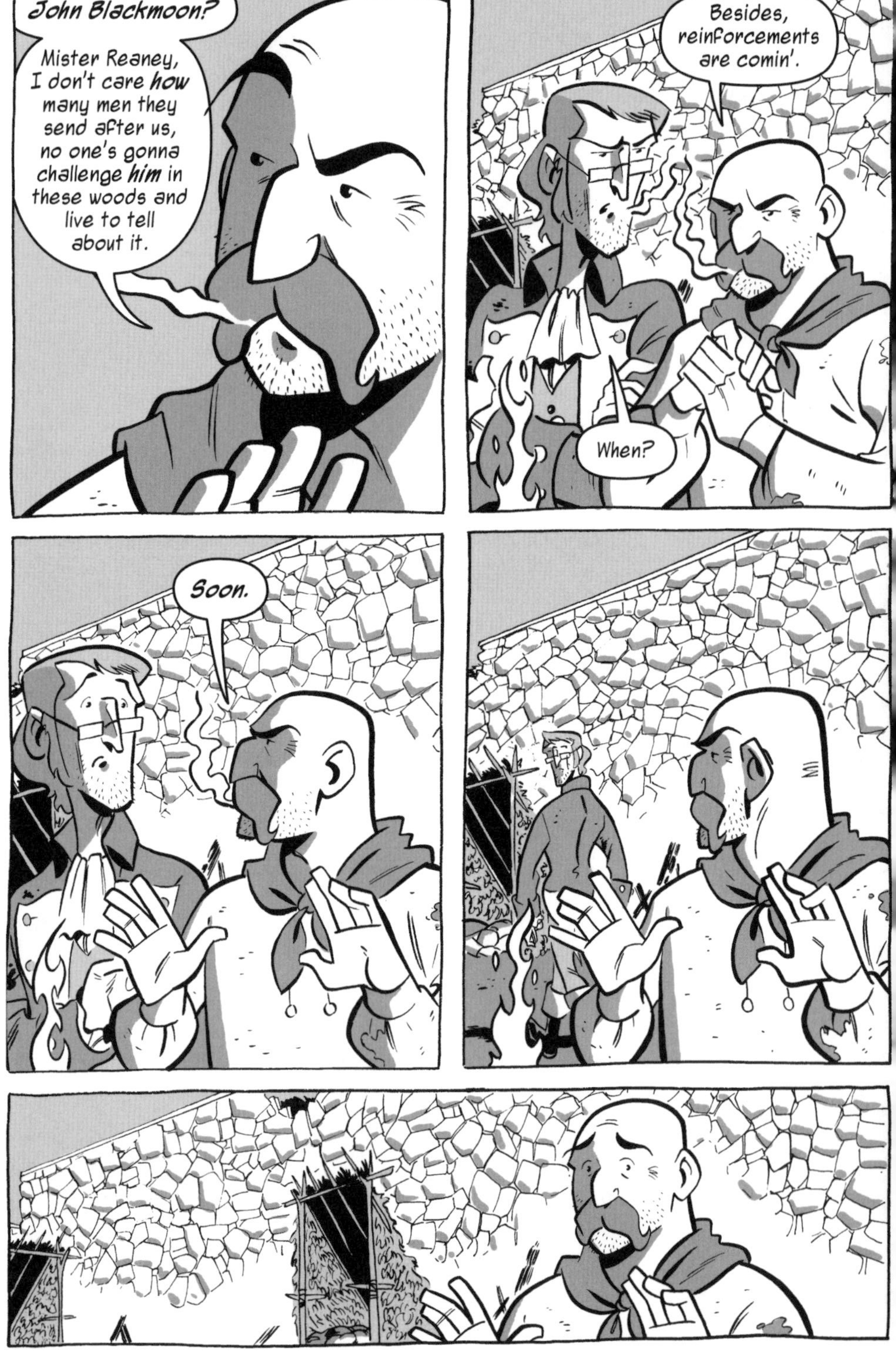
John Blackmoon?
Mister Reaney, I don't care **how** many men they send after us, no one's gonna challenge **him** in these woods and live to tell about it.
Besides, reinforcements are comin'.
When?
Soon.

CREEEEAAAK!
Steady, lad.
Here.
Drink.

They've agreed to let me see you every other day or so. But I don't have long.

What's your name, son?
F-Fletcher.

Templeton Fletcher.

You're the nephew of our Governor.
Yes.
But for the love of God, don't let Montglave know it. He'll kill me.

You have a cousin here at the Fort, you know. They haven't killed **him**.
I know. I was there when they caught him.

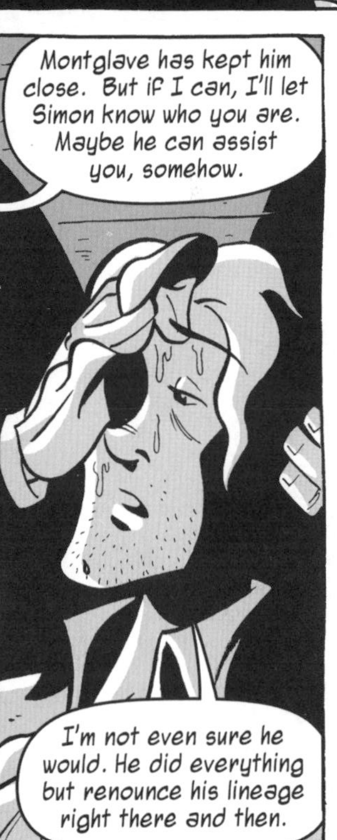
Montglave has kept him close. But if I can, I'll let Simon know who you are. Maybe he can assist you, somehow.
I'm not even sure he would. He did everything but renounce his lineage right there and then.

Simon is a hard lad, but a canny one. I'm sure he only did what was necessary to spare his life.

Just as **we** have done.

Reverend...?

Yes?
Will we go to Hell, you and I?
For hanging those men?

The Lord wants us to *live*, my son. Otherwise we'd be hanging right beside them.
He spared us because He wants to test us. ***Why***, I don't know, but I fear that was only the ***First*** part of the test.

But did we *pass* the first part?
I don't know.
I hope so.

Do you think we'll survive the second part?
I've prayed for wisdom and guidance, lad, and think I may have found some...
And what's that?

That the Lord helps those who help themselves.

Heh.
There's not much I can do to help myself in *here*, Reverend.
I'm just going to keep praying that my uncle will rescue me before Montglave has me killed.
Son, I don't even know whether your uncle is alive or dead.
If he *is* alive, he doesn't even know you're here.

Prayer is good. But don't despair. Remember what St. Ignatius said...
..."Act as if ye have faith, and faith shall be given to you."

Reverend, you forgot your--

Oh, silly me! So I have.

Let me just slip that back into my satchel.

See you in a few days, lad. And remember...

...The Lord helps those who help *themselves*.

Now, tell me, Simon...

...What ever became of your *mother?*
A Cree princess, was she not?

You knew my mother?
I did, briefly.
You remind me of her, in your way. Dark, and proud.
She is dead, I presume?

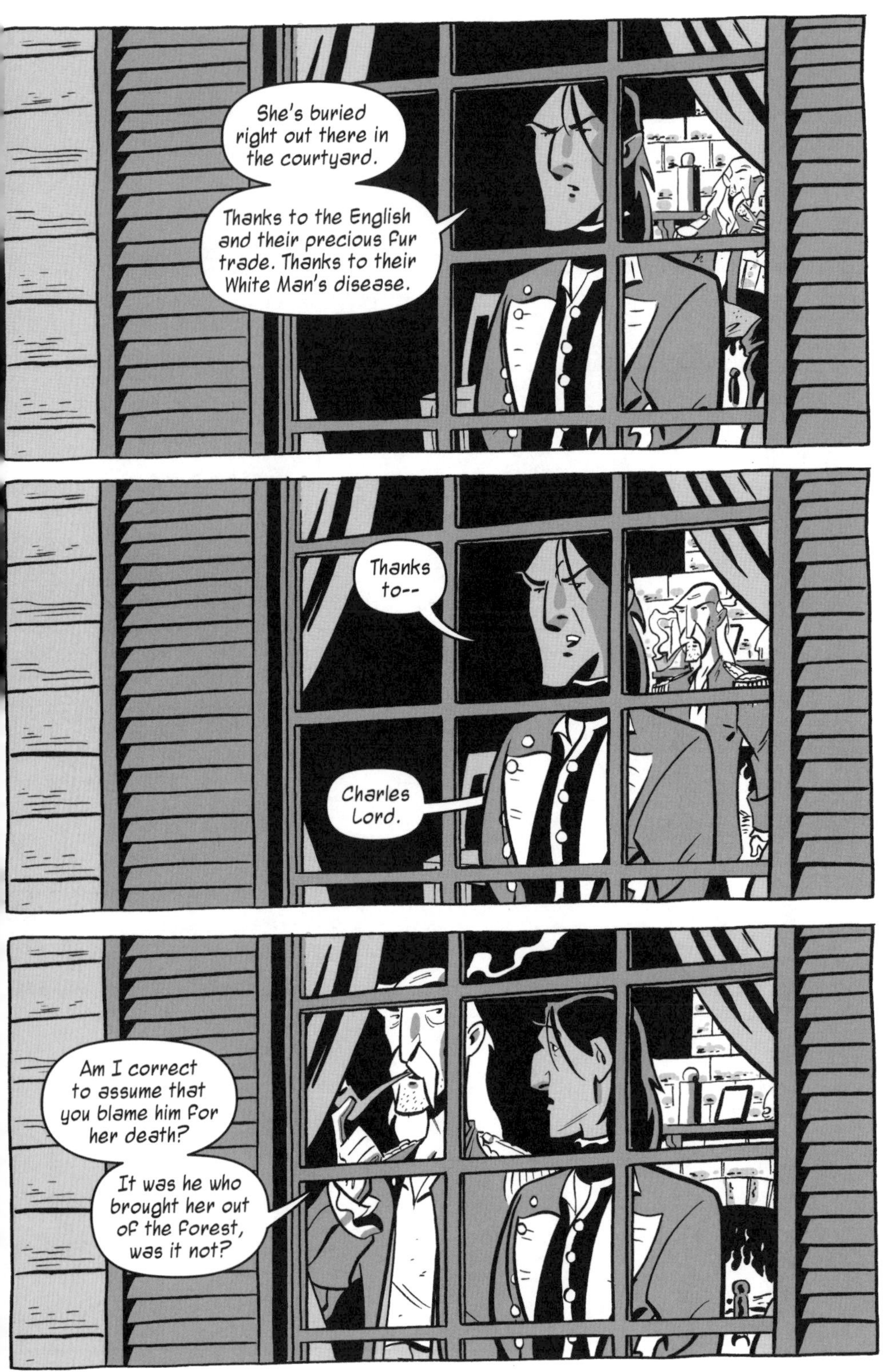
She's buried right out there in the courtyard.
Thanks to the English and their precious fur trade. Thanks to their White Man's disease.
Thanks to--
Charles Lord.
Am I correct to assume that you blame him for her death?
It was he who brought her out of the forest, was it not?

Tore her from her ancestral home and forced her to live in this artificial community carved out of the trees, rock, and swamp?
You think she would have been better off had she never even **met** Charles, non?
Even if it meant you were never born?
I **curse** the English in my blood. It is my **shame**.
Yet you continue to live here in their very headquarters!
The Cree won't have me.

Speak up, garcon, my advancing years have had a terrible effect on my hearing.
I said the Cree won't have me.
Of course not. You are too White to be Red, and too Red to be White. Is it not so?
You are right to be ashamed of such a malediction. The English are boorish, lazy dullards, without an ounce of the sophistication of the French.

You Europeans are all the *same* to me. English, French-- what difference does it make?
Whites are a race of fools, killing each other over *rodent skins*.

Now, now. You are going to hurt my feelings with that kind of talk.
I think you will find we Frenchmen much more understanding than our English counterparts.

But I will let you in on a little secret, jeunne homme...

I am not just here for the *furs*.
KNOCK! KNOCK!

Qui l'est?

J'ai avec moi le chirurgien Anglais, Monsieur. Il veut voir le garcon.*
Pour quoi?
* "I have the English surgeon here, Monsieur. He wants to see the boy."

Now Monsieur Montglave, you promised that I could visit the prisoner every few days. To ensure his health.
Prisoner?

There are no prisoners here. Simon is free to come and go as he pleases.
Is he?

You won't mind if I take a quick look at him, then...
It is up to ***him***, of course...
Come in, Reverend.

How are they treating you, lad? Getting enough to eat and such?
Plenty.

Well, medecin, does he meet with your approval?
He appears to be in one piece...

Let's try to ***keep*** him that way, hmm?

Je ne comprend pas pourquoi Montglave veut que nous pourchassions le restant des Anglais.*
* "I don't understand why Montglave wants us to hunt the rest of the Englishmen."
Ne mourront-ils pas si nous les laissons ici quelques semaines de plus?*
* "Won't they just die if we leave them out here a few more weeks?"
Je ne compterais pas dessus. Un des hommes que nous pourchassons est *Lord Charles*.*
* "I wouldn't count on it. One of the men we're hunting is *Charles Lord*."

Le meme Lord Charles que celui qui a survécu seul un hiver a Digges Island?*
Le meme.**
* "The same Charles Lord who survived a winter alone on Digges Island?"
** "The very same."
Merde!
Mais c'est un menuisier accompli! Ses hommes et lui pourraient etre en train de **nous** poursuivre!*
* "But he's a master woodsman! He and his men could be tracking **us!**"
C'est pourquoi j'espérais que vous ne partiriez pas comme une troupe de trompettistes Espagnols...*
* "All the more reason why I wish you men weren't going off like a bunch of Spanish trumpeters..."
Que--?!

SNAP!

Your friends are all *dead*, Frenchman.

T'ose men were not my friends.
No matter.
You work for Guerin Montglave, don't you?

I t'ink we bot' know t'e answer to t'at, Cristinaux.
And you know who *I* work for?
I do.

Good.
I want you to think about that on our way to the English camp. I want you think about the fact that when we get there...

...You're going to wish *you* were dead, too.

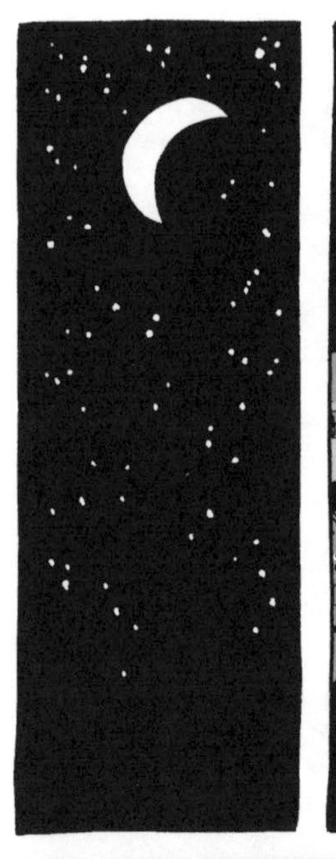

Is that a boat out there?

Where?
There.

It's him.
It's the Governor.

Hallelujah!
Now we'll finally run those bloody privateers off!
How many men does he have with him?

None.

Simon:
The young man they are holding in the gaol is your cousin, Templeton Fletcher of Aberdeen. He is not being treated well. If you can find a way to assist him, please do so.

RIIIIP!

ZZZZZZZ
!

The Annotated

NORTHWEST PASSAGE

Interlude

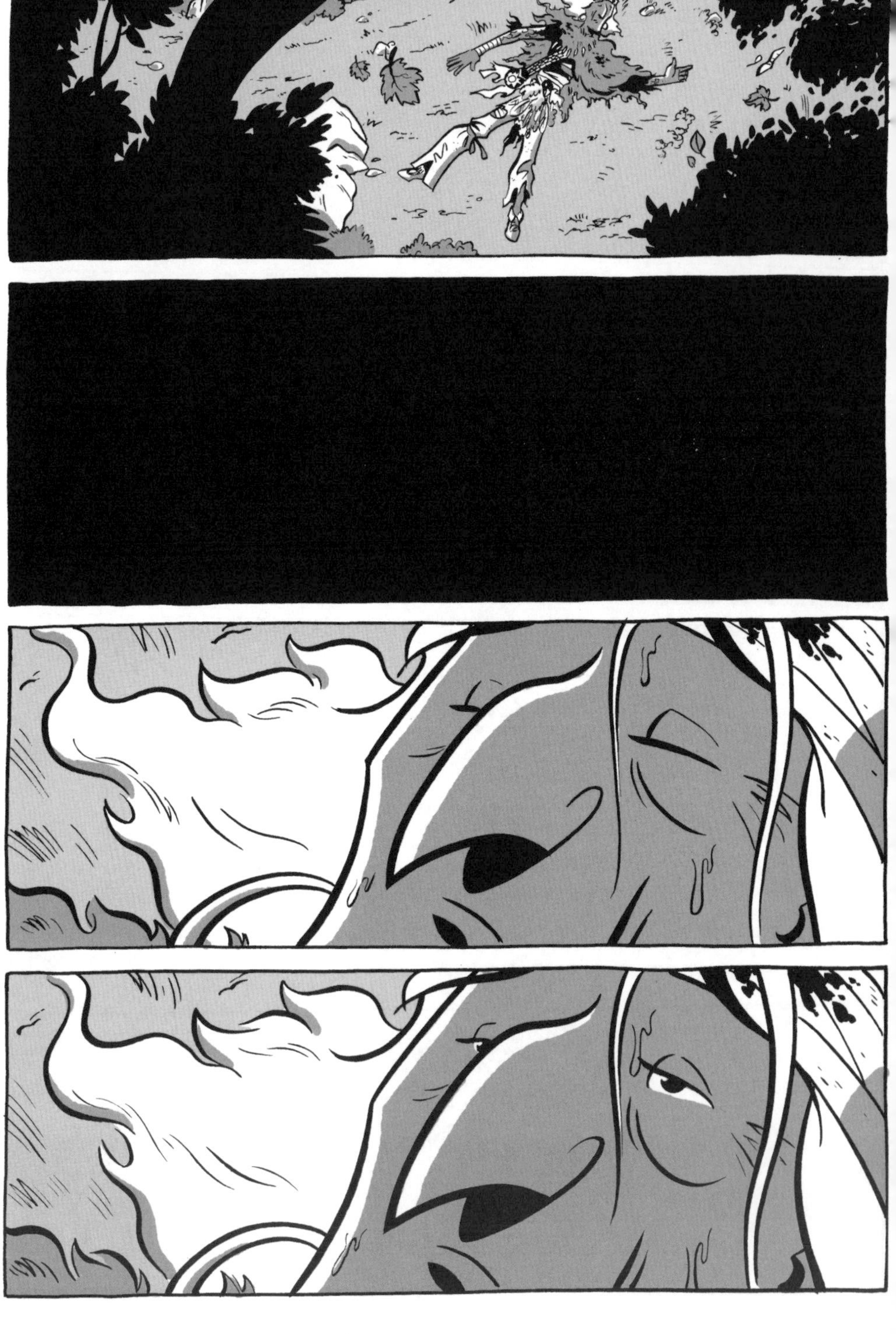

The Annotated

NORTHWEST PASSAGE

Chapter 5

"Truth and Lies"

Wake up.

They let you walk around *unguarded?*

So we're supposed to be *cousins*, then?
Seems that way.
I'm digging a *tunnel*, at night.
I should be out of here in another *three days*.
But you'll only be out of your *cell*. Getting over the walls and past the watchmen is another matter.
I have a *plan*.
But I'm going to need *your* help.

Remove the blindfold.
Parlez-vous anglais?
I do.

You know who I am?

Yes.

Your surgeon...
Kirby?
Yes. I captured 'im **myself**.

And t'ere is an 'ostage from t'e **Maid Marian**. Young fellow, smart as a carrot.

His name?
I do not know. I would **tell** you if I did.

And t'ere's a **half-breed.**

I do not know who 'e is, but Montglave seems interested in 'im for some reason.
Three men.
Three out of more than a **hundred** between the ship and both forts.
Bloody **animals**.
Who knows how many **Cree** slaughtered, as well.
I did not know about **t'em**.
I beg your **pardon?**

'E never told us about t'e Cree camp. 'E sent an 'andpicked group of men to track some **shaman**, but t'e rest of us never knew what t'ey were doing.
You're **all** madmen, to have followed that hedge-pig!
T'ey are **madmen**.

T'ere has been more bloodshed t'an many of us would have liked. Most of us just signed up for a share of t'e profits from t'e **furs** we would capture.

We were not expecting a **war**.
Expected or not, Frenchman...

...You **got** one.

May I ask, Simon, what was to happen to you when Charles returned to England?

He gave me a job here, as a clerk.
You weren't to go **with** him?
No.

HA!
I can just imagine your response when he asked you, though! You must have been on the high ropes!
I probably **would** have been.
He never asked.

His own **son?**
He would have known what your response would be, surely, to living in that nation of pale ghosts?
To leaving your homeland? To leaving your **mother**, half a world away in a white man's grave?

Still.
It would have been nice of him to **ask**.
Of **course** it would have.
My professional quarrels with the man aside, that just seems ***outrageously*** discourteous.

The question now is what you will do when *I* leave...

What do you ***mean?***

All of these **furs** I have liberated from English hands need to make their way back to France, garcon.
I will be leaving just enough men here to defend the place during the winter and spring, and will return as early next summer as I can manage...
...If for no other reason than to be here before the **English** ships which will certainly come.
But I have a long voyage **in between**.
And I enjoy our **chats**.
You would **work** on the ship, of course. The more hands the better. But you would also be my **guest**.
I know how much you **despise** Europe, but many a cold heart has warmed upon its first sight of Paris, the most **romantic** of cities.

I would even introduce you to our King, *Louis the Well-Beloved*, and the people of my country would *celebrate* you as the striking composite of cultures that you are, not as a mongrel to be *kennelled* and *shunned*.

I--
I--

I know what you will say.

I just wanted to *ask*.

Qu'est-ce que nous avons ici, Monsieur Lambert?*
Des commercants, Monsieur. De la Nouvelle-France. Ils viennent d'arriver.**
* "What have we here, Mr. Lambert?"
** "Traders, sir. From New France. They just arrived."

Nous avons entendu dire que la Compagnie venait de la Baie. J'ai pensé que nous pourrions apporter nos fourrures ici, au lieu de les apporter jusqu'à Montréal.*
* "We heard rumours that the Company had been driven from the Bay. Thought we might bring our furs here rather than haul them to Montreal."

Bon.
Donnez-leur un bon prix pour leurs fourrures et demandez-leur de les charger sur le navire.
Je veux etre sorti de ce satané pays avant la fin de la semaine!*
* "Give these men a fair price for their pelts and have them load them onto the ship. I want to be out of this God-forsaken country by week's end!"

Oui, monsieur.

They've got *Simon*, and the *Reverend*. Possibly my *nephew*, as well.

So, they're *alive*, at least.
I wouldn't wager on that being the case for much *longer*.
We can't wait for next summer, and help that may not arrive. If we're going to take the fort back, we have to do it *now*.

All due respect, sir, but that was gonna be a tall order even if you *had* come back with the canoe full of extra hands we'd hoped fer.
There're scarcely more'n a *dozen* of us, after all.

If this prisoner can be believed, their numbers are less than *half* what they left New France with.
And it sounds as if *most* of them are operating only out of fear of Montglave and the few who are *loyal* to him.

Surely you don't think they'd surrender to a force that's half their number!

No.

But if we can demoralize them still ***further***, they'll be more likely to ***turn and run*** than ***stand and fight***.

Governor, ***please!***

He's got my ***son***, Duncan! You don't ***understand***, you're not a ***father***.

These men will follow you ***anywhere***. You know it as well as I.

But they're ***blacksmiths*** and ***carpenters*** and bleedin' ***mail clerks***, not ***soldiers!***

They are ***now***, old friend.

They are now.

"On the third night from tonight, I expect to be free of the prison.

"And *disguise* myself among the fur stores that Montglave's men have been loading onto the ship.
"I don't really *need* to escape...
"They're going to *roll* me out of here."
Now, here's where *you* come in.
On the fourth night, you'll meet me on board. Come alone if you can, but if they send a guard with you...
Kill him.
Right.
Now this is important. *You're* going to have to let me out of the barrel.

"They stack them one atop another in the ship's hold, sometimes three or four high, and there's no sense in hoping that I'll be on ***top***."
Once I'm ***free***, we'll drop one of the lifeboats.
I don't know how fast just two of us will be able to ***row***, or even where we'll go. But as long as it's away from ***here***--away from ***Montglave***--we'll be safer.
I'll take my chances with the elements.
And maybe, if fate is ***with*** us, we'll be reunited with your father, my uncle.
I just wish we could bring the Reverend.
Don't worry about Kirby. They need a ***doctor***.
Most of them are Roman Catholic and wouldn't kill the chaplain, anyway. As long as he doesn't cross Montglave, he'll live.

You understand what you need to do?
Yes.
Good luck to you, then.
"To both of us."

The Annotated

NORTHWEST PASSAGE

Chapter 6

"Faith and Desperation"

Je me sens en veine aujourd'hui. Comme si je pouvais empocher une dizaine de perdrix.*
* "I feel lucky today. Like I could bag a dozen partridge."

Vraiment? Eh bien moi, je vais en avoir dix-huit!*
Dix-huit? Aussi bien dire un mil....**
* "Is that so? Well, I am going to get eighteen geese!"
** "Eighteen? You might as well say a thous--"

CRAK!

Tireurs!

TIREURS!*
CRAK!
CRAK!
* "Snipers!"

Fermez cette barrière! Il y a des tireurs dans les arbres!*
* "Close the gate! There are snipers in the trees!"

Lord.

Rapidement!

I know you're out there, Charles!
SHOW YOURSELF!

I'll do nothing of the sort, montglave!
You've got the fort, but these woods are OURS!

Any man so much as sticks his toe out the gate is going to get it SHOT OFF, unless it's one of the prisoners marching his way out!

It is PRISONERS you want, is it?
What makes you think we HAVE any? You know me, Charles--"only good Englishman is a dead one," eh?

Because we have one of our OWN!

That would be René de Cuthbert, I suspect!
I was beginning to wonder what happened to him! A good fighting man, but terribly critical of the way I decorated my new mess hall!

You'll pay fer what you done in there, Montglave! Mark my words, you will!

HO-HO!
Is that DUNCAN MacDOUGAL I hear?

I should have known you would be along! Still riding the coattails of our betters, are we?
Enough talk, Montglave!
We propose an exchange! Yours for ours!

Allez chercher le garcon de la palissade.*
Pourquoi?!
* "Get the boy from the stockade."

Faites ce que je vous dis!
Si je peux le convaincre de libérer Cuthbert, nous connaitrons leur position.*
* "Just do it. If I can convince him to release de Cuthbert, we will know their position..."

Et là, nous pourrons leur transmettre la bienvenue, comme il se doit.*
* "And then we can send them a proper welcome."

Nous sommes pratiquement prets à larguer les amarres.*
* "We're just about full up in here...time to sail soon."

J'aimerais bien pouvoir partir. Ici, l'hiver sera notre mort.*
* "I wish I were going. Winter here will be the death of us."

Je me demande si les filles à Paris sont aussi belles qu'à ma souvenance...*
* "I wonder if the girls in Paris are as beautiful as I remember..."

CLANG!
Qui est là?*
* "Who's there?"
Is someone t'ere?
Simon?

I'd have your answer, Montglave! What's it to be?
Monsieur Montglave!

Le garcon a disparu!*
Quoi?!
* "The boy is missing!"

Allez chercher l'aumonier!*
* "Get the chaplain."

Non. Allez chercher Simon.*
* "No. Get Simon."

Where are you 'iding, Englishman?

You'll drop off t'e perch when Guerin Montglave gets 'old of you, coward!

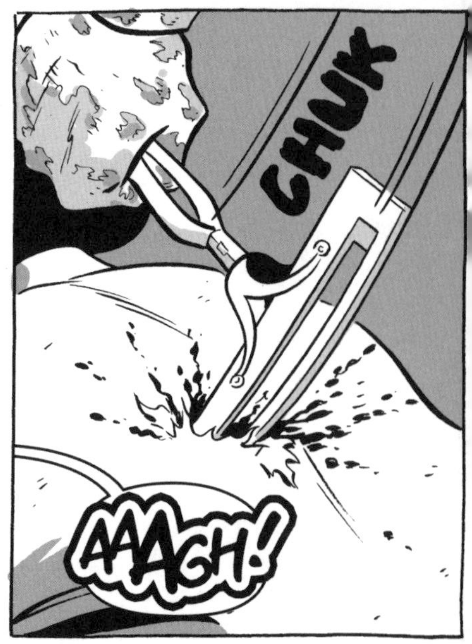
CHUK
AAAGH!

Do not send me back, Monsieur Lord.
Excuse me?

Please.
Do not send me back. 'E will kill me.

Release me. I-I will fight for you.
You would fight against your countrymen?

Montglave is a monster. He ordered my friend Amaury killed. 'Anged all those men...
Anyone who would be led by that devil is no countryman of mine.
I'll not believe the word of a Frenchman.
Especially one with so much blood on his hands.
You'll be dealt with in time, and not released beforehand.
Besides, there won't *be* any prisoner exchange. Montglave's only stalling, trying to figure out how to turn this to his *advantage*...

Hold 'im, Aalart.

I am not even going to *take* 'im to Montglave.
I am going to send 'im to t'e diet of worms right ***now***.

Now, now...

It's about time you rusty guts learned that this type of behaviour just isn't appropriate for polite society.
Now *drop* it.

Charles, you will be glad to know that your siege has been successful!
I am sending out one of the prisoners!

One isn't good enough, Montglave!
We know you've got THREE! We want them ALL, or we'll see to it that you starve in there!

That hardly seems fair, Charles! If you are offering but one hostage, then it seems I should offer just one, as well!

Besides, it is my understanding that this one has some SPECIAL SIGNIFICANCE for you...!

That son of a bitch.

What say you, Charles?

Is HE a desirable enough trade for a traitorous Frenchman you barely know?

Charles, please!
WINTER is coming, can you not feel it?
The moment you build a fire, I will send every cannonball in this fort raining upon it!

You may have cut off our food supply, but WE have SHELTER! When the snow comes, which of us do you think will outlast the other?

I have heard your terms, vieil homme, now hear MINE!
Call off your ridiculous rabbit hunt or I will KILL them all!

I will kill them ALL, Charles! You KNOW I will!
Run, boy.
Blood and 'ounds, why doesn't he run?

Is there any part of you that does not think I would rather kill them and risk starving than to let YOU WIN?

And I will start with THIS one!

Do you hear me, Charles?
Simon!

Right here and now, let us start the bloodshed with HIM!

SIMON!

Cock and pie!

Grab yer flats and sharps, men...
IT'S ALL OF US OR NONE OF US!

Voilà!

FEU!

BOOM!

BOOM!
POOM!
POOM!
POOM!
POOM!

Jesus, Jack...
I said drop it.
He *didn't.*

We should *never* have listened to you!
"Turn the canoe around," you said. "We'll make for the Bay, unload our furs, and take a quick look around for prisoners."

You *did* promise we wouldn't get involved, Jack...
Did you just want to *stand* there while they *killed* him?

Now they're going to kill *us*, fool!
HA!
They may kill *you*, mate, but let's not give them *too* much cred...

It's *him*.
The old loggerhead is *really* trying to *do* it.
Trying to get himself *killed*, by the look of things.

He won't make it past the cannons.
We'll need to *distract* them.
How?

GUNPOWDE

POOM!
POOM!
POOM!

BOOM!

We're *finished*, Duncan.
Let me get a look at that *shoulder*.
We're *beaten*.

We'll come back next summer with a *ship*, sir. And *Marines*. And we'll--
Dammit, Duncan. The prisoners will be *dead* by then! They may even be dead by *now!*

Hold still.

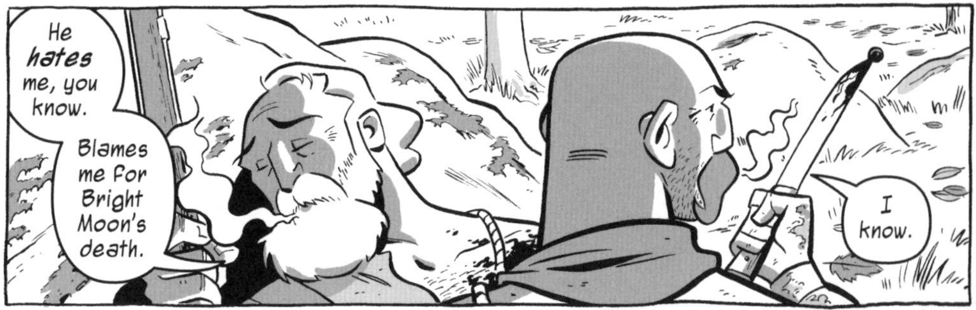
He **hates** me, you know.
Blames me for Bright Moon's death.
I know.

The boy's **wrong** to blame you. You brought Simon and his mother here to **protect** them.
And look at the good it's done! All I did was make it known exactly where he could be **found!**

I've been a **terrible** father.

You **sure** about this, Jack? A whole season's worth of furs...
We already **got** paid, Speck.
GUNPOW

Why don't we just fire on the fort with the ship's cannons?
With just **seven** of us to man them? How many shots do you think we'd get off before they **sink** us?

It's this or **nothing**. Then we'll swim ashore and join the attack.
Assuming you don't blow us all to **hell** in the process.

No **promises**, lads.

I almost didn't come **back**, you know.
What?
When I went to find **Jack**.
He offered to take me with them to Montreal, then into the **interior** next spring.
He wants to find the **Northwest Passage**. He just uses the fur trade as an excuse to **explore**.
Like **we** used to.
You wouldn't have gone with him.
I almost **did**.
But you **didn't**.

I was *tempted*. Tempted to let Simon, and you, and all the others just--
Enough, Charles.

What?

I said that's enough of yer *blabber*.
I haven't got time to listen to listen to you *tune yer pipes*, and neither does anyone *else*.

This is the hero of half of England?
There's a lot that son of yers doesn't understand, and maybe you should've been straight with him from the *beginnin'*. But the time fer *cryin'* about it is *done*.

You may not think much of yerself at the moment, and maybe you and Kirby can sit down with a bleedin' *Bible* and work it all out, should you both *survive* this.
But right now there're a dozen men, and three more inside that fort, whose *lives* depend on what you do *next*.

And we're waitin' fer CHARLES LORD to show up and LEAD, goddamn you!

KA-BOOM!

What the hell was *that?*
With any luck, a *diversion*
Follow me.

MAID MARIAN

Arret!*
* "Stop!"

Do **not** open t'at gate!
It's **over**, son.
Why don't you drop your weapon and ask God's forgiveness for what you've been a party to here?

I am **warning** you, Reverend.
Step **away** from t'e gate. **Do** it, or I will...

...

Ils ont percé nos lignes, messieurs!
Préparez-vous à attaquer. Ils nous ont joué un tour!*
* "We've been breached, men! Stand and fight! It's a trick!"

Did I not say that the curse of my people would be upon you?

"YOUR PEOPLE?"
I see only YOU, shaman! A wounded old ghost!

Look again, White murderer!

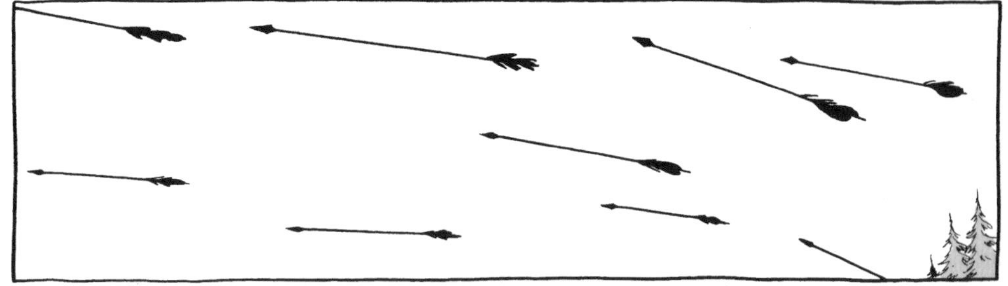

LOOK AGAIN!

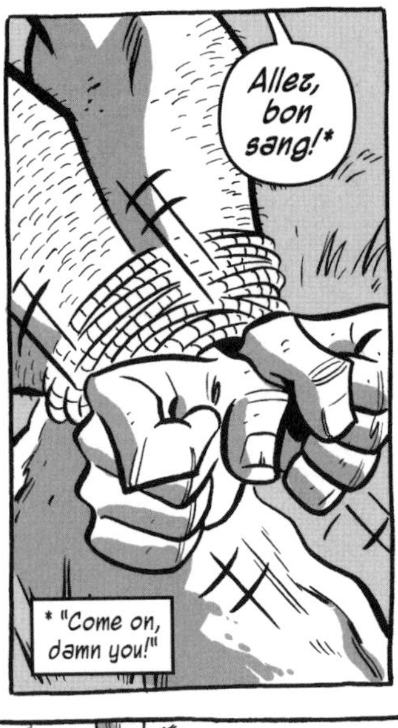
Allez, bon sang!*
* "Come on, damn you!"

UFFF!

Duncan...?

DUNCAN!

Easy,
old man.

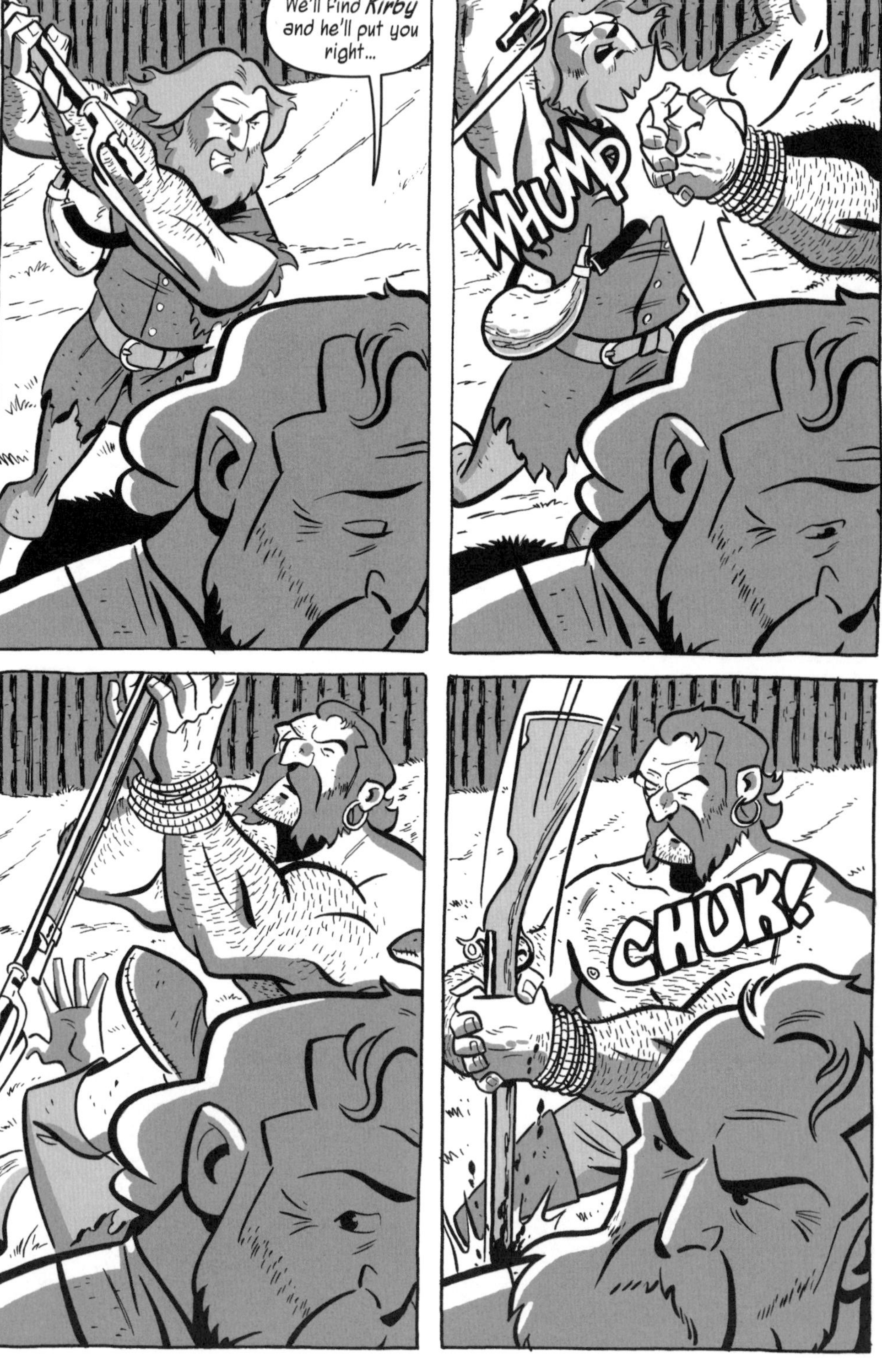
We'll find *Kirby* and he'll put you right...
WHUMP
CHUK!

Hold still.
SWISH!

My thanks, Frenchman.
Now, where are they holding my son?

Simon...!

I *knew* you'd betray me, you *bastard!*
Where are you *hiding?*

Come out and fi--!

Where have *you* been hiding, cully?

Keeping you *alive* has been more trouble than it could *possibly* have been *worth*.
Let him *go*, Montglave.

Uncle!

"Uncle," is it?
I *wondered* why these prisoners seemed so awfully *precious* to you, Charles.

Any *other* relatives at the fort I should know about? A *third cousin*, perhaps?
You look like your *mother*, boy.

Keep your *distance*, Charles.
And if I *don't?*

ZEV!

POOM!

Heh heh.

CRACK!

Where *is* he, you devil? Where is my *son?*
You have *neglected* that boy, Charles.
And what is more, I think you *know* it.

WHERE IS HE?!

I'm *here*.

I thought I wasn't a *prisoner*.
Remember?

If you are speaking of the unfortunate matter at the **gate**, believe me when I say that **no harm** would have come to you, nor would I have handed you over to them.
Don't believe **anything** he says, Simon! He's a **snake**...
I **meant** what I said yesterday, **fils.**
I would have fled **already**, but came back here instead in the hope that you would still **accompany** me.
What kind of **Banbury stories** has he been filling your head with, lad? He's--
Don't move.

What?
I said *don't* *move.*

You wouldn't kill your own *father--!*
No.
He *wouldn't.*
Time to empty the bag, Charles. You have never *told* him, have you?

Have you?

T-told me *what?*

We've *done* it! The rest are *surrendering!*

That may be enough for *you an' me*, Speck, but the Cree will keep fighting nonetheless.
Why?
We've already won. The fort is *ours*.

These men destroyed their *village*. Killed their *families*.
Killed their *children*.

There hasn't been *enough* killing?
Not just *yet*, friend.

Not just yet.

Many years ago, Simon--before you were born--I established a trade relationship with an *inland tribe*.
"They were the *Opaskwayak*, led by your *grandfather*, Chief Straight Arrow.
"In exchange, he offered me in marriage his middle daughter, *Bright Moon*.
"There was but one *problem*.
"Much to my surprise--and your *grandfather's*--she *refused* me.
"It seems she was enamoured with an *English trader* who had once rescued her from a *bear attack*.
"Not just *any* English trader, mind you...
"...but my *chief rival*."

Now, I am not one for the heathen rituals of the savages...
The fact that she would not have me in whatever devil-worshipping ceremony the Cree take for a wedding bothered me not one penny's worth.

"But your mother, as I have said before, most assuredly had her charms.

"So before I left the village, I took something from her.

"And from Charles, too.
"Something she might have wanted to give him herself, if you take my meaning."

Years later, I hear that Charles Lord has become the governor of Fort Newcastle, with an Indian bride and a half-breed child in tow.
And I have to wonder...

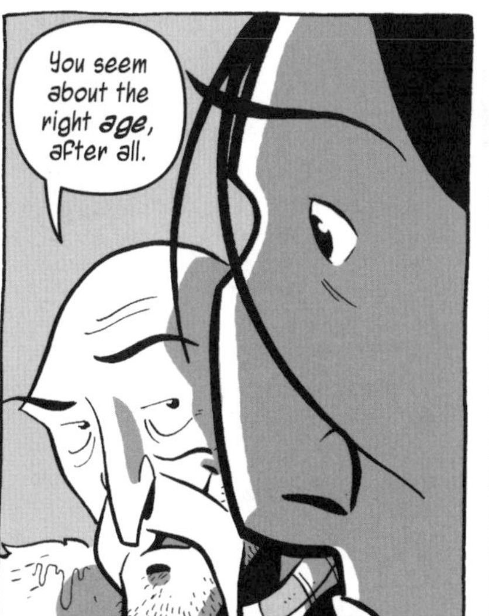
You seem about the right *age*, after all.

Now, is *that* a lie, Charles? A *"Banbury story?"*
Or have I done what you would *not* by telling the boy the *truth?*

You...

You *raped* my mother?

Such an *ugly* word, Simon!
She was only doing what her father wished to secure our ***business*** relationshi--
Simon.
Son, I--
Shut up.

I am *not* your son.

The Annotated

NORTHWEST PASSAGE

Epilogue

Charles...?

Hm?

The men need you.
They want to know what happens **next**.

Have I brought them back together just to see them **dead** before the **spring?**

I believe your Reverend Kirby would say, "The Lord helps those who help themselves."
And what would the **Great Spirit** say?

The Great Spirit would add, **"And others."**
"And others."
Indeed.

They **need** you, Charles.
Come **inside**.

End.

The Annotated

NORTHWEST PASSAGE

Annotations

Pages 3-8

The first thing a lot of people (especially readers outside of Canada) probably say to themselves when they open to the start of this story and begin reading is, "where the heck is Rupert's Land?" For the record, Rupert's Land was the territory granted by England s Charles II to the Hudson's Bay Company in 1670, named in honour of his cousin Prince Rupert, the Company's original governor. The grant gave the HBC complete control (and thus a lucrative fur trade monopoly) of all lands that drain into Hudson's Bay. A 17th century European monarch could have had no idea how large a percentage of the Earth's surface he had just given away: the expanse of Rupert's Land included what is now northern Quebec, much of northern Ontario, all of Manitoba, nearly all of Saskatchewan, the south end of Alberta, and large portions of the Northwest Territories and Nunavut.

I struggled right to the end with pinpointing the exact year in which *Northwest Passage* would be set. I finally settled on 1755 because it was the year before The Seven Years War (known in the U.S. as the French and Indian War) broke out. The Seven Years War is significant in North American history because it's during that conflict that the English capture New France (now Quebec), which eventually leads to the creation of Canada. 1755 is also well into the period during which the HBC—as we'll learn later in the story—eschewed exploration and expansion, content to let their men linger at Bay-side posts. It's a time of real complacency that is about to be shaken up by violence and change—much like what occurs in the story.

A number of people have remarked that this opening sequence reminds them of the beginning of Michael Mann's 1992 film version of *The Last of the Mohicans*. I've seen the film, but not since its initial release (it

was, in fact, the first movie my future wife and I saw together when we began dating that year,) so it's doubtful I was influenced by it while creating this scene. It should be noted that there's a similar shot in *The Fellowship of the Ring*, when the orcs are chasing our heroes down the river. When it comes down to it, people jumping over a log while running past a stationary camera probably isn't all that original. Whoever I swiped it from, it seems to have made for a good opening—people tell me all the time how much they enjoy this chase.

Pages 10-18

The sample script that I sent to Oni Press when I was pitching *Northwest Passage* actually began with this scene, which was originally meant to be the opening. The chase scene in the prologue was initially part of the flashback in chapter two. It stayed that way until the final draft—one of the last script changes I made to the volume one script was to cut and paste those six pages from the middle of the script to the beginning, and label them "Prologue." It was one of the most important decisions of the entire writing process. It saved Eagle Eye's back story from becoming too long, and also provided a much more exciting opening. But more importantly, it created a structure in which the prologue, interlude, and epilogue could be told from the point of view of a third character, Eagle Eye (as opposed to the main story, which is very much Charles's and Fletcher's.)

Fort Newcastle is a fictionalized version of York Factory, which was the HBC's North American headquarters for nearly three centuries. It seemed like any available visual reference for York Factory was from its later incarnations, though it was burned by the French in 1782 and later rebuilt and added to, so I made it look like Fort William. Fort William was actually a North-West Company (the NWC was the HBC's rival, for a time) depot in what is now Thunder Bay, Ontario. But there was a lot of available reference—Fort William is actually still standing, after some restoration, and acts a tourist destination—so it made sense to use it as a model.

York Factory changed hands between the English and French six times in its history, which demonstrates how fervently European nations wished to control—or prevent others from controlling—the fur trade in North America. It's hard to believe from our 21st century vantage point, but there was enough money in beaver skins to go to war over. *Northwest Passage* depicts a fictional struggle, but similar events happened on the Bay with surprising regularity.

Radisson and Des Grosseilliers (whose name I badly misspelled as "DeGrossiers" in the original edition of this book), mentioned by Kirby on page 18, are pivotal figures in Canadian history. Pierre-Esprit Radisson and his brother-in-law, Médard Chouart Des Grosseilliers, were French explorers who were so furious at being fined for unlicensed fur trading in New France that they went to the English with a plan for trading into Hudson's Bay from the north, bypassing the French completely. This led directly to the formation of the HBC. Radisson, in particular, is one of the most colourful and daring rascals to ever blaze his name across history. He lived among the Iroquois and Mohawk as a youth, changed allegiances between the English and

French numerous times, and ended his career with a price on his head. I've tried to allow his adventuresome spirit to live on in the character of "Quick" Jack Prince (whom we'll meet later in the tale.)

CHAPTER ONE – "ARRIVALS AND DEPARTURES"

PAGE ~~FIVE~~ SIX

Panel One. Large establishing shot of Fort Newcastle, from the water. It is early evening. The fort is a large one, with a palisade, behind which the roofs of several wooden buildings--including a watchtower--can be seen sticking up. The flag of the Hudson's Bay Company flaps atop a tall flagpole, identifying this fort as belonging to England. A trail of smoke curls into the sky from somewhere within. Outside, many boats (York boats and canoes) have been pulled up on the shore. Just to one side of the fort is a small Cree encampment…tepees, etc.

CHARLES (within): Gentlemen! Thank you, one and all, for joining me this evening.

PAGE SEVEN

1 **Panel Two.** Wide shot of the interior of Fort Newcastle's crowded mess hall. Most of the occupants of the fort are gathered, drinks in hand, listening to a speech being given by Governor Charles Lord, who stands on a table with his own glass raised. Lord is in his mid-forties, bearded, and seems slightly uncomfortable in his more formal dress. Behind him, a fire roars in a large fireplace.

CHARLES: ~~As we all know, the supply ship that's expected in the next few days brings with it your new governor, Sir Walter Hargrove.~~ As you all know, I'll soon be stepping down as the Company's overseas governor… …and that the next supply ship brings with it…

2

3 **Panel Three.** Cut to an exterior shot of two hunters, muskets in hand, walking carefully through the brush. It's cold enough that they can see their breath, a stark contrast to the warmth of the previous shot. Though they carry the meagre spoils of the day's hunt—small animals, mostly rabbits—they are still alert, hoping to bag a deer before returning to the fort.

6.

7.

Musicians behind him?

Pages 19-20

I've been asked a few times whether I named the character of the chaplain as a tribute to legendary comic book artist Jack Kirby. I didn't, at least consciously. I just like the name. (It never comes up in the story, but for the record, Reverend Kirby's first name is Morton.) Jack Kirby is someone whose work I respect immensely, but I don't consider him a great influence on my own work. If I were going to pay tribute to someone in this respect, I'd have named the chaplain "Eisner."

A few people were bothered that Kirby came off a little too much as a stereotypical close-minded religious fanatic in the early chapters. What can I say? He's a chaplain in the 18th century! And while I can't deny that Charles's views toward religion in this scene mirror my own, I think that later events in the story demonstrate that Kirby is, in fact, one of the heroes, not simply someone for Charles to dress down whenever I feel like it. Like all of the characters, Kirby has an agenda—his is just worn on his sleeve.

Panel three of page 20 is, for my money, some of the worst drawing in the book. Charles looks like Robert Crumb's "Keep On Truckin'" guy.

Pages 21-23

This scene was a late addition. It was, in fact, the very last change I made to the first script before I started pencilling it. I was half-way through writing volume two before I began drawing volume one—and it was becoming clear that Simon was a much more important character in the story than I had originally thought. In my original outline, he was the ineffectual son of Charles Lord, who stayed behind during the capture of the fort, messed up Fletcher's escape plan, and in the end had his true lineage called into question. He still does all that stuff, but as I got into chapters three and four, the relationship between Simon and Charles took centre stage, and stayed there. I'd started off writing a story about the value of loyalty, friendship, and sticking together through tough odds. As often happens when you're writing, though, the theme began to narrow and come into sharper focus. What I was *really* writing about, it turned out, was loyalty, friendship, and sticking together *as it applies to fathers and sons.*

I shouldn't have been surprised. Just before I pitched *Northwest Passage*, my first son was born. It's clear to me now how much of my hopes and worries about being a father are mixed up in this tale, not to mention elements of my relationship with my own father, and grandfather. Despite being set two and a half centuries from my own time, this is really a deeply personal work, as close to autobiography as anything I'll likely ever write.

That being the case, Simon couldn't just all of a sudden become the centre of attention mid-story. He needed a lot more set-up in the first volume than he originally had, a rationale for why he might possibly be swayed to Montglave's view of things. So I wrote this scene, which I think establishes where he's coming from at the beginning of the story fairly efficiently.

Pages 24-30

There's a lot of exposition in this scene. I wanted to establish some of the history of the period, cement Charles's relationship with Duncan, introduce (in flashback) the other members of Charles's "old guard," and also set up the concept of the Northwest Passage, one of the book's central themes. The only way to do a lot of this is through conversation, but I don't really do "talking heads." I prefer my characters to be *doing* something, even while engaged in lengthy conversations. So I used this as an opportunity for Charles and Duncan to take a stroll through Fort Newcastle, letting the reader get a feel for its size, character, and armaments before it gets ravaged by not one, but *two* successful raids. I always like it when a scene can accomplish not just one or two things, but several things at once.

As I mentioned in the acknowledgements in volume one, most of the historical reference regarding the search for the Northwest Passage and the politics of exploration versus commerce in the HBC comes from Peter C. Newman's excellent books *Company of Adventurers* and *Caesars of the Wilderness*. I urge anyone interested in the history of Canada to read them.

I felt for certain that page 27—a splash with most of the major characters together, in their glory days—was going to be the first piece of original art to sell from this book. But as of this writing, it's still sitting here in my office. Shows you what I know. It also features the only glimpse we've had so far of Barclay and Watt, two of Charles's men who don't reappear later. Watt is the bespectacled one gathering wood far in the background. Barclay is asleep under the canoe because I didn't want to be bothered designing a character that would likely never be seen again.

Pages 31-33

As I was drawing the stern of the supply ship for the first time, it occurred to me that the vessel was going to need a name. I couldn't think of one off the top of my head, so I asked my wife, "hey, what do you think is a good name for an English supply ship?" She immediately replied, "the *Maid Marian*." I thought naming it after Robin Hood's famous damsel in distress would work great, especially considering how much trouble this particular ship finds itself in later. It was also a tip of the hat to the European legends and folklore that *Northwest Passage* is meant to be a "Canadian-ized" version of. So I wrote "Maid Marian" across the back of the ship. Sometimes it's just that easy.

When I was writing this scene, I also got hung up for a while on what book Fletcher would be reading when we first meet him. *Hamlet* almost seemed like too obvious a choice. But like the famous Danish Prince, Fletcher has some serious daddy issues, so it seemed more appropriate than anything else I could think of. Plus, I think it helped add to the humour of the scene that Warwick and McPhee (two supporting players whom I was very sad to have to kill off) hadn't heard of something that's not only famous, but the most famous thing ever written in the English language.

The line about Shakespeare being "the yardstick against which society measures its literacy" is something one of my university drama professors used to say, and which has always stuck in my head. It's kind of pretentious…but also kind of true.

Pages 34-40

When I began working on this project, I had just seen *Master and Commander* (one of my favourite films), and was excited that I would get to draw a ship. Little did I know what I was getting myself into—all those ropes nearly made me blind! The *Maid Marian* is based on Captain Cook's ship the *Endeavour*, which was from approximately this era, and was a cargo ship. Being such a famous ship, there was also plenty of visual reference available. So many people have built detailed models or even full-scale replicas of the *Endeavour* that this ended up being one of the easier subjects to research.

This is another exposition-laden scene, which could also have been "talking heads"—my first draft had Fletcher and Hargrove talking across a desk in Hargrove's quarters—but which I was eventually able to come up with something more interesting for. I read something (can't remember what right at the moment) about a retired naval captain who could never get out of the habit of walking the decks of ships at night, and immediately gave that trait to Hargrove. Moving the conversation to the deck of the ship not only gave me the chance to establish the layout of the *Maid Marian* better, but it also meant that Hargrove and Fletcher could be the ones to spot the boats containing Montglave and his men (in my first draft, they simply heard the commotion above and ran upstairs to see what was happening.)

I miss Hargrove. He was a fun character to write, and a fun character to draw. Too bad he's dead.

Pages 42-46

A few people have commented how much this scene sticks out from the others, on account of it being so static. I don't think they mean it in a negative way. At least, I hope they don't, because this is one of the scenes in the book I've always been proudest of, design-wise. (Although if I knew I was going to be reusing the same background seventeen times, I sure wish I'd done a better job drawing it. Yikes.)

The idea of two characters sitting at either end of a long table as an external demonstration of their internal distance from each other is something I stole from *Citizen Kane*, of course. But I've tried to expand on it by simply holding the same shot for longer than is comfortable, through all of the awkward pauses, to give the reader a glimpse of what Charles and Simon are actually like when they're alone together. In that way, for all of this scene's (mostly) unchanging, arm's-length detachment, I actually think of it as being one of the most intimate. When Kirby comes in later and blocks Simon from view, it's about how Simon *feels*, even though we no longer see him.

That the small talk between Charles and Simon is about the weather is more than just an indication of their discomfort with each other. It's an attempt to show how focused Charles is on what's going on outside the fort, rather than inside it. Any time in these early chapters that Charles wasn't doing anything else, I'd have him look out a window (as he does here) with a vague sense of longing. He's like a caged animal. Outside, he's a hero. Inside, he's an administrator, and the father of this mopey kid. It's hard to blame him for being distracted by the outdoors. We'll find out later, of course, what not looking inward will cost him.

The objects hanging on the walls above their heads are astrolabes, which are ancient astrological navigating devices. Given that Charles was an explorer, I figured it natural that he'd be interested in collecting this kind of stuff. And if readers want it to interpret their presence in this scene as an indication that Charles and his son are "lost" to each other, I won't complain.

Pages 47-49

There was little visual reference I was able to find regarding surgical tools and techniques from the 18th century. One of the few things I did find was a picture of the portable medicine cabinet that appears in this scene. Being the only medical-related detail in the room, you'll notice how much I try to make use of it: I sneak it into the background whenever I can, and even go in for a close-up on page 48. I really wish I could have found more medical accoutrements to put around the scene, but you use what you've got. I'd rather do nothing than have to fake it.

In the pencils for page 47, panel four, I originally had Charles clasping his hands around *front* of himself…until someone pointed out that from the angle we're viewing it at, it looked like Charles was about to perform a certain bodily function onto the bed. Eagle Eye's expression did nothing to prevent this interpretation. When it came time to ink this page, I moved our hero's hands safely around back. It's always good to have a fresh pair of eyes look at the pages!

Many of the details about day-to-day life in this era, such as the fact that they would have celebrated St. George's Day (April 23rd) with a shooting match (which Charles mentions on page 48) come from Michael Payne's book *The Most Respectable Place in the Territory: Everyday Life in Hudson's Bay Company Service at York Factory, 1788-1870,* which was an indispensable reference during the writing of this book.

Pages 50-52

I don't know if I really ever made clear that the reason the captain thinks the men they've "rescued" are English is because Montglave is wearing the coat of one of the HBC officers from Fort Duchess of York (which, as we learn later, he and his men have recently sacked.) I think I was expecting to explain this in more detail later on, but never did.

The original art for page 51 is owned by former Oni Press sales and marketing director Maryanne Snell, who also owns a piece from my previous book, *Scandalous.* It's always nice to know you have fans at the company that signs your cheques.

Pages 53-66

This is a long scene, one of the longest in the entire story, and it's hard to believe now that it used to be even longer. As I mentioned in my notes for the prologue, there used to be six extra pages of chase scene here, which just made it drag, and kept us away from Charles for far too long. It works a lot better as it is.

The eye lines in panels two and three on page 53 have always bothered me, because it appears that Charles is looking at Kirby, even though he's talking to Eagle Eye. These are the kinds of things you notice after the book's already in print, of course, and not being able to change them makes you crazy.

The "conversation" between Eagle Eye and the eagle on the cliff was one of the very first scenes I imagined for this story. The whole idea of him climbing up there and being warned of the attack on the village *as it's happening* seemed inherently dramatic to me. The mysticism is a little at odds with the earthiness of the rest of the tale, but I thought it was important that we see what Eagle Eye can do. Nobody has ever complained to me that they found the presence of "magic" in the story distracting, and I was careful to place this sequence during a flashback, so that we pretty much have to take Eagle Eye's word for what happened up there. I'm not making a claim one way or the other about whether or not Eagle Eye's "powers" are real—though Charles and Montglave clearly believe that they are (the latter going so far as to send men to kill him before he can foresee the attack on the supply ship.)

Many of the details of Eagle Eye's communication with "the Grandfathers" are taken from, and inspired by, *Cry of the Eagle: Encounters with a Cree Healer* by David Young, Grant Ingram, and Lise Swartz. It's a scholarly look at Aboriginal medicine, and the views and techniques of Russell Willier, a Woods Cree who is a part of that ancient tradition.

The art style used for Eagle Eye's vision is inspired by a number of Native American artists, most notably a painter named Leland Bell. His work can be seen in a variety of places online—I encourage you to look him up.

The splash on page 66 was nearly used for the cover of volume 1. I always thought the image of the looming foreground supply ship bearing down on the tiny background fort pretty well summed up the action of the first book. In the end, I ended up going with something more character-oriented, but I still really like that shot.

Pages 67-71

It should be pointed out that ceilings in ships weren't nearly this high. But I decided that I couldn't sell Montglave as an imposing and impressive enough figure to be Charles's equal if he was hunched over during his entire introductory scene. So I fudged the height of the room so that he could stand in all his haughty uprightness. When historical accuracy and dramatic necessity clash, drama wins every time (for me, at least.)

Another good example of dramatic necessity is "the Hinterland River," which Fletcher refers to on page 70. There's no such river with that name anywhere in the world (at least that I'm aware of,) but I didn't want to take a real discovery away from a real-world explorer and give it to my fictional one. So I made one up. I figure that as long as I'm fictionalizing the names of forts and HBC governors, there's no harm in fictionalizing the name of a river or two.

Montglave is one of my favourite characters. It's really fun to write and draw someone so vain and oily. Although he's dead by the end of this story, it's my intention that as the series continues he will reappear in flashbacks and stories set in earlier timeframes (I'm hoping to be able to occasionally work backwards and fill in some of the characters' histories… more on this later.)

When people refer to *Northwest Passage* as an "all-ages" book, I have to wonder if they're skipping scenes like this one, in which dozens of people are shown to have been massacred. Sure, the historical setting is kind of educational, and my drawing style is simple and "animated," but the body count in this story is pretty high. This isn't Disney's Frontierland—things get pretty dark, especially in second and third acts.

Don't get me wrong: I'll take any audience I can get, and if younger readers are enjoying the book then I welcome them to it. I don't think it will harm them to know that people in the past often butchered each other for the same silly reasons that they do today. But I certainly wasn't aiming at the youth market. Although I wanted *Northwest Passage* to mythologize Canada's history to an extent, I didn't want to "clean it up" for anyone. Canadian history, as taught in schools, is largely about politics and shipping routes and such, and downplays the exploration, the danger, the adventure—and yes, the violence—that's often been glossed over because it's not how Canadians generally think of themselves. I wanted to do undo that, at least to the extent that a mere comics series can. Human history is soaked in blood, and I think that to depict otherwise is misleading at best, and irresponsible at worst. Tom Stoppard expressed it best in *Rosencrantz and Guildenstern are Dead*: "...We can't give you love and rhetoric without the blood. Blood is compulsory. They're all blood, you see."

Pages 73-78

When the story was published as individual volumes, this scene was the beginning of volume two. At the time I didn't worry about beginning this chapter in a different time and place than had ended the previous one—there was, after all, six months between volumes, and it was natural that readers would expect a new "beginning" each time. Now that the story has been collected, I fear they might find it a jarring transition. As much as these first three *Northwest Passage* volumes are meant to be a single narrative, I tried to put those breaks to the best use I could, and I think that the serial nature of its original publication actually helped the storytelling somewhat.

Reaney is a character I wish I'd set up better in volume one. He really just kind of showed up out of nowhere in the second volume (out of the necessity for having someone for Duncan to butt heads with as the de facto leader of the survivors of Fort Newcastle,) and disappeared just as quickly once we got to volume three. It seems pretty sloppy to me now. This was my first professional writing experience, and while I'm proud of my effort on the whole, there are things like this that stand out as being pretty amateurish.

The old cliché about choosing between your characters being like picking between your children isn't really true, at least for me—my favourite *Northwest Passage* character is Duncan, no contest. Many readers have told me the same. So I really enjoyed writing this middle act, where he steps forward and becomes a character that we follow for a while, at least until Charles returns. The bit on page 75 where he is revealed to be the one who helps Reaney to his feet is one of my favourite character-revealing moments in the whole story.

Pages 79-81

There are quite a few scenes throughout the story that begin (or end, or both) with shots of the moon, as this one does. As evidence of how obsessive I can be regarding details of setting, I actually worked out the moon phases as a way of (hopefully) not only demonstrating the passage of time, but reminding people of the different time frames between one story thread to the next. The entire story takes place over about eight weeks, but the different narrative tracks move at different speeds. For instance, the journey of Duncan and the other survivors to Fort Duchess of York takes a matter of days, while Charles's journey inland to find Quick Jack takes three weeks in either direction. Yet I "cut" between them as if they were happening concurrently. I'm not certain anyone noticed or cared, whether it was a help or hindrance to setting the story's "clock," but if nothing else it's a notable sign of my lunacy (pun intended.)

I decided to re-use the hunters from volume one in this scene, because I thought it was important that we recognise some of the survivors, and that the "name" characters weren't always simply leading around a group of generic tag-alongs. In fact, nearly all of the survivors are background characters that appeared in the first volume at least briefly. I also figured it would be more dramatic if the two men that John Blackmoon gets the better of during his introduction had been previously shown to be competent woodsmen in their own right.

Speaking of John Blackmoon, the only thing that gave me pause when the decision was made to divide this lengthy tale into three separate volumes was the fact that he (along with Jack Prince, the story's other real "action hero") wouldn't be introduced until the second one. Both got a brief mention in a flashback appearance in volume one, but I figure that their late entrances to the main story are something that your average creative writing professor would consider a mistake. So be it. It seems to have worked, and it's not the only place in the story where I deliberately disobeyed "the rules." In fact, I broke a big one in the very next scene.

Pages 82-91

As I mentioned previously, *Northwest Passage* was my first professional writing experience. In an attempt to make myself feel more confident, I read a few writing books before I began, including Robert McKee's much-talked-about *Story*. All were unanimous in insisting that the inciting incident (in the case of *Northwest Passage*, it's the capture of the fort) not be set up in flashback. Clearly, I've thumbed my nose at that here. It just felt right to do so. For one thing, I didn't want the third act *re*-taking of the fort to seem redundant. I also consciously wanted the violence in the first two acts to occur, as much as possible, either off-screen or in flashback. That way the final battle, when it came, would have as much impact as possible. I have as much respect as anyone for the principles of story structure, but when it comes down to it, you've got to go with your instincts, even if it goes against convention.

I've actually found most of the books on writing I've ever encountered to be full of theoretical bluster, and not particularly helpful when it comes to actually putting words on paper. The only one that I regularly turn to is Ronald B. Tobias's *20 Master Plots and How to Build Them*. It's a simple, practical, and helpful manual on how to construct classic story types. In fact, the original outline for *Northwest Passage* largely came about as my attempt to combine Tobias's "rescue" plot with his structure for an "escape" plot.

I'll never forget how long it took me to draw page 85. It doesn't look all that more crowded than other pages, but there's actually close to sixty characters on that page. It's one of the many times when Scott Chantler the artist resented Scott Chantler the writer.

Duncan's remark on page 88 about things being "a bit chalky with France" is a bit of foreshadowing of the coming outbreak of The Seven Years War. Although the official declaration of war didn't come until 1756, many modern scholars now date the war from 1754, to include the colonial skirmishes that led to the wider war. I plan to eventually address the Seven Years War more directly in the pages of *Northwest Passage*, but not until at least volume seven. It will take a while for these characters, living as remotely as they do, to catch wind of what's happening in the wider world.

Which, naturally, begs the question of how Duncan knows about the increased tensions between England and France. In our age of instantaneous information, it's hard to imagine what it must have been like for the Bay men, whose only source of news was the supply ship that came once a year. It's probably pushing it to think that the 1754 supply ship brought word of the French attack on Fort Trent in mid-April of that year, although tempers were already flaring in the Ohio Country as early as 1753, so it's not unrealistic to think that Charles and his men might have received some inkling of it.

I thought it would bother people that I didn't better flesh out the character of John Blackmoon. I lay out a fairly compelling back-story for him in this scene (he's an Englishman living as an Indian, used to be a Company employee but isn't anymore, etc.) then don't mention it again for the duration of the story. I hoped he wouldn't come off as having been dropped into the story simply for the sake of being some sort of secret weapon that kills as many "bad guys" as possible. A few people who have written about the series have compared him to Hawkeye from *The Last of the Mohicans*, but he's actually inspired by Canadian historical figures like Etienne Brulé, Grey Owl, and to a lesser extent Pierre-Esprit Radisson. Either way, nobody's ever complained about it, so I think I got away with it. He doesn't have as much to do in this story as I'd have liked, but I wanted to at least set him up well, as we're going to learn much more about this mysterious character as the series progresses. Plus, I thought it was important to show that Charles had at least one "son" who remained steadfast. His simple nature and easy loyalty make a nice contrast with Jack's personality.

The Louisbourg mentioned by Duncan on page 91 was a French fortress on the eastern tip of Cape Breton Island in Nova Scotia. It was captured twice by the English, though I've imagined a third (unsuccessful) assault by privateers here. Blown up after England's seizure of France's North American colonies, Louisbourg was eventually rebuilt, and is now a national historic site.

Pages 92-94

It's purely for the sake of convenience that many of Montglave's men are able to speak English. It took me a while, though, to figure out how to deal with the accent. Montglave speaks English perfectly—it seemed to me that he wouldn't have come off impressive enough if he talked in some sort of broken second language—but for the rabble of thugs and hired guns who make up his men, I wanted to represent the distinct sound of English as spoken by the French. I generally dislike when accents are spelled out in comics dialogue—the results are often hard to read, if not downright insulting. I'd rather have done nothing than to have characters spouting things like "zis" and "zat." I was struggling with how to represent such speech in volume two when I read Chester Brown's *Louis Riel* for the first time. He used a subtle yet effective approach to the French Canadian accent in that book: simply dropping the letter H. So I "borrowed" that particular technique here.

Pages 95-99

Page 95 is one of my favourites. Believe it or not, the death of Charles's servant is the first killing that we actually see "on-screen" that isn't a flashback. So I wanted it to be memorable in some small way.

This scene is, of course, a crucial one. As I wrote earlier, this was the point in my first draft when I was beginning to realise just how much the Charles/Simon relationship was central to the plot. I also like it because it's one of the few times I was able to pull off having the audience know something that the characters don't. On pages 98 and 99, Simon can't see Montglave's face, so he doesn't know (as we do) the extent to which his captor is toying with him with these questions. I'm pretty happy with the way this scene turned out. It foreshadows a lot of what's to come.

Pages 100-104

Here we come finally to the introduction of that rascal "Quick" Jack. It felt strange to have a major character first appear a hundred pages into the story, but the point, of course, is that this is the one of Charles's "sons" who is estranged. We see in him where Charles's relationship with Simon is headed.

"Made-beaver" was the standard barter currency of the Canadian frontier. It referred, simply, to a quality adult beaver pelt. Traders valued their goods accordingly. A brass kettle was worth one made beaver. A pistol, four. A rifle, ten or twelve. And so on. The Cree are correct that Jack is trying to cheat them by claiming the HBC would want three made-beaver for twenty fishhooks. According to HBC tallies from the era, they valued the fishhooks equivalent to one made-beaver.

Cree translators don't exactly grow on trees, so the Native dialogue here was actually lifted from a Cree language website. The scene was built around numbers and simple phrases that the site listed translations for, with English responses that made clear what the Indian characters had said. I think it worked quite well. Of course, the Web being what it is, it's entirely possible that the translations are less than accurate—they might actually be asking for ham sandwiches, not fishhooks. So far, though, I haven't encountered anyone who would know one way or the other (if anyone reading this happens to be an expert in Cree language, please contact me, as I'll have use for you when writing upcoming stories.)

I cringe at my bland depiction of the Cree here. This is one of the few times in the story where I had to draw a group of Natives, and I resorted to simply putting them in loincloths (despite it being autumn) with some feathers in their hair. They're all so generic looking. At this stage in the art process, though, there just wasn't enough time to investigate the culture thoroughly enough to give everybody in the crowd an individual look. A future storyline is going to be set among the Cree, so I hope that at that time I'll be able to properly immerse myself in the necessary research to really make those characters into *characters*, as well as delve further into the language issue I mentioned above.

Jack's statement that "it's three weeks to the Bay from here" is my attempt to set up the distance that Charles has travelled to find him. Jack and his men weren't just around the next tree. They're well inside the interior (it's not important to the story, but in my head these scenes are taking place near the northern tip of Lake Winnipeg.) My original concept for the story had a lot of action taking place during Charles's trip—we'd have seen him wrestling bears, hunting moose, climbing cliffs, carving a canoe out of a tree trunk, and all sorts of other "man versus nature" kinds of things. But it became clear rather quickly that that wasn't the story, that it was possible just to have him show up in a buckskin shirt and know that he'd transformed into the "old" Charles over the course of the journey.

Pages 105-108

Fort Duchess of York is based on the historical Prince of Wales's Fort, which was the HBC's northernmost outpost (though I've cheated a bit by having such a fort exist in its finished form in 1755—Prince of Wales's Fort was constructed intermittently over forty years, and not completed until 1771.) It was unique among the posts in that it was built of stone and housed a battery of forty cannons, meant to be a defensive bastion at the northern edge of the HBC's domain (it didn't work...the French captured and subsequently blew it up in 1782.)

I call panel three on page 106 "my Tony Moore shot." Tony and I shared a booth at Wizard World Chicago in 2004, and over the course of the weekend I learned all I'll ever need to know about drawing rotting corpses. *The Walking Dead* was starting to become very popular, and I must have watched him do about a thousand zombie sketches for people. I love Tony's work.

Pages 109-110

Guerin Montglave almost comes off as charming in the scenes he's appeared in thus far, but this, of course, is where we learn what a black-hearted villain he really is. The mass executions of this middle act caused more than a few people to comment how much darker the second volume was than the first, and are one of the things that prevents it, as I wrote earlier, from being as family-friendly as many people expect.

It's not without historical basis, however. In 1642, after accepting the surrender of an English fort on the Saint John River, Charles de Menou d'Aulnay offered one of the prisoners his life if he acted as a hangman for all of the others. The prisoner complied, and the others were strung up, one by one, in front of the wife of the fort's governor (the governor was at a different post at the time of the attack.) I first read about this terrible incident in Harold Horwood and Ed Butts's *Bandits & Privateers: Canada in the Age of Gunpowder* during my research phase for *Northwest Passage*, and it stuck with me long afterwards. I thought it was just the kind of treacherous brutality that Montglave would be capable of, as well as being a suitably bleak spiritual challenge for Fletcher and Kirby to face. It eventually became the centrepiece of the second act, and provided most of the necessary motivation for nearly everything that happens at Fort Newcastle from this point forward.

Pages 111-115

I felt I owed the reader an explanation of how Charles was able to find Jack among the vast wilderness of what is now Canada. I hope the one that appears on page 111 is sufficient. Basically, because Jack is an independent trader and not affiliated with the HBC, he must haul his furs all the way back to Montreal every season to sell them to the French. The northern part of North America a one large system of lakes and rivers (which is what allowed the fur trade to exist in the first place,) but since the days of Radisson, a standard route had been established that carried traders back and forth across what is now Ontario and the Great Lakes. Charles would, naturally, be familiar with this route. So it was really just a matter of heading Jack off along the way. (As an aside, I'm planning on canoeing a part of the historic fur trade route—the French River, from Lake Nipissing to Georgian Bay—not long after this book sees print in the spring.)

By 1783, independent traders like Jack had banded together to form The North West Company. Beyond its adventuresome origins, the HBC mostly gave up any activity but collecting furs at trading posts on the Bay (much to the fictional Charles Lord's chagrin, as we learned in chapter one.) For The North West Company, though, exploration was part of the job, as they penetrated to the deepest corners of the frontier in an attempt to cut the HBC off from its customers by going to the Indians, rather than having the Indians come to them. The HBC enveloped The North West Company in 1820, but the competition of the intervening years did much to rekindle the era of exploration (including renewed interest in finding the Northwest Passage.) I didn't want to bog the book down with all of this history, but I hint at the beginnings of the rivalry on page 112.

This is another scene I like the design of quite a bit. My goal was to never have Jack and Charles in the same panel, as a way of representing the "wall" between them. I wasn't sure it'd be possible to maintain without it calling too much attention to itself and coming off as a gimmick, but I think it worked pretty well. When laying out a page, it really helps to have some sort of overarching creative idea to hang your decisions on.

Punishments at the forts were usually severe because, as Charles says on page 114, these men lived in what is now northern Manitoba, while the nearest English courtroom was probably someplace in Pennsylvania. And trading behind the Company's back was a serious offence. From what I've learned, punishment was left up to the governor's discretion, though the common ones are listed by Jack on page 115: whipping, fining, shorting of rations, and imprisonment. I've had Charles choose the lash, because it helps the image of Jack as the child who got spanked.

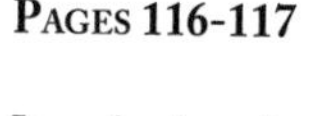

Pages 116-117

It took a lot of writing and re-writing to get these scenes to "cut" together in just the right way so that we get Montglave's view of "discipline" juxtaposed with Charles's. You've got two storylines—Charles's and Fletcher's—which have, at this point, diverged as far from each other as they're going to, the events of each scene separated by three weeks and hundreds of miles. Yet they needed to meet up here on an important thematic note. I tried it many different ways until I arrived at something that worked. This was as hard as it got for a first time writer. Script-wise, I was over the hump from this point on.

The shot of Montglave handing Fletcher and Kirby the rope on page 117 was one I had in mind from the moment I added the hangings to the plot, and is meant to recall the shot of the HBC officer handing Charles the whip in the previous scene. One of my favourite panels in the story…it gave me chills when I first thought of it, and it still does.

Pages 118-121

The audience doesn't know it until the end of volume three, of course, but the battle for Fort Newcastle is actually won in this scene. It's won in the final panel of page 118, when Charles apologizes to Jack. This is a major breakthrough for Charles, the stern father figure who we've seen has trouble communicating with his son. It's this simple act of contrition that leads to Jack's eventual decision to come to Fort Newcastle, which in turn is the only thing that allows Charles's rash and ill-considered attack to succeed. I knew by this point, of course, that the story was *really* about Charles mending fences with his "kids"—so I made that panel the largest on the page as a way of hinting at its significance. (Jack's reaction is subtle and guarded, but you know something has shaken loose, because as of the next page, he and Charles suddenly begin appearing in the same panel as a way of marking the turning point.)

It should be noted that the first white man to reach the Athabasca Country was actually Peter Pond, in 1778, but I felt it was well within Jack's character for him to exaggerate his accomplishments somewhat.

Pages 123-124

As I mentioned earlier, I originally envisioned this story to be more one of the survival of the remaining Company members. There were meant to be whole scenes depicting what Duncan and the men were doing to stay alive in the wilderness. But, again, that ended up not being the story. I incorporated all those ideas into this simple scene, which demonstrates both the passage of time (being colder now than when we last left these characters in chapter three) and the less-than-ideal conditions that they've had to endure.

That said, I hate the drawing in this scene. Given that the same shot is repeated eight times, I should have come up with a more interesting background than the stone wall. It distracts too much from the foreground characters.

Pages 125-131

While I was writing, I could never shake the feeling that I was concentrating so much on developing Charles's story that Fletcher's was getting short shrift. This scene changed that. The addition of the hangings (and Fletcher's role in them) gave me the opportunity to take the character to his breaking point, and also provide the motivation for him to want to escape. This is where his story really picks up steam.

This scene also adds some needed depth to the character of Reverend Kirby. As I mentioned in my notes for his introduction, he came off as something of a caricature in the first act. Here he retains the beatific smile and attitude that only the most determinedly religious can manage, but also demonstrates the depth of his understanding of just how bad things have gotten, and sneaks up on the reader with the initiative he displays in planting the seeds for Fletcher's escape. Kirby's an interesting character, one who always surprises me with what he does next.

Don't ask me what the medical implement is that Kirby gives Fletcher to dig his way out with. Finding reference on that kind of stuff was, as I've previously mentioned, difficult. It's an antique surgical tool that I found a drawing of, but I have no idea what it's used for, or even if I've drawn it the correct size.

I think there may be some confusion about what the hole in the floor of the cell is. There's only one reason to have a hole in a prison floor: it's the latrine. It may have thrown people that it just appeared out of nowhere, though. I wish now that I'd established it earlier by showing it here and there in the background throughout the scene.

Fletcher's soul-searching over the hanging of the prisoners isn't over. It will, in fact, be the focus of volume four of the series (which I'm outlining as I write this commentary.)

Pages 132-138

I drew the early part of this scene with the idea in mind the "camera" would move (or the characters themselves would) so that Montglave appeared to be circling Simon, disorienting him. He'd be on panel left in one shot, panel right in the next shot, etc. I think I ended up disorienting *myself*, though (not to mention my editors) because when the first printed copies of the third volume arrived at my home, I was horrified to see that Montglave's pipe disappeared for a whole page on page 136, and then reappeared on page 137. That's been fixed for this edition.

The inter-breeding of Native people with European settlers eventually gave rise to one of Canada's recognized Aboriginal peoples—the Métis. Simon clearly feels completely alone and outcast here, but within a century the dissatisfaction he's voicing in this scene will be the dissatisfaction of an entire culture within Canada, giving rise to the North-West Rebellion of 1885. I tried to write Simon's dialogue as if planting the seeds for that future struggle. (For a complete and historical look at the North-West Rebellion and its still-controversial leader—in comics form, no less—I urge you to read Chester Brown's excellent non-fiction graphic novel *Louis Riel.*)

Pages 139-143

Aside from the hangings, this is probably the most talked-about scene in the book. Obviously, I'm moving the story forward here with René's capture, but mostly I just wanted to show what John Blackmoon can really do. People also responded to the design of it, with the "camera" holding steady and the mercenaries one-by-one disappearing from view. It's the way I envisioned the scene from the very beginning. I like when action scenes are able to maintain some kind of viewpoint and tell you something about a character, rather than just having the reader's attention be pulled around all over the place as it would in a kung-fu movie or the like. Of course, sometimes you *want* the fighting in your story to seem chaotic and random, but in this instance I wanted to demonstrate the quiet, deadly efficiency of the character by having the killing be over nearly before the reader (or anyone in the party that's being attacked) has even realised it's begun.

The quote about Charles Lord surviving a winter alone on Digges Island (a small island at the northern tip of Hudson Bay—almost at the Arctic Circle, and definitely not somewhere you'd ever want to spend a winter) is something I just plugged into the script as being something impressive-sounding that Charles could have done in his career, but I've actually been thinking of filling out the story and using it in the series at some point. You never know what's going to send things off in a new direction. We'll see.

On page 143, René refers to John as "Cristinaux," which was what the French called the Cree. I hoped it wouldn't confuse people, but no one's ever mentioned it, so I assume people who didn't know the reference were able to guess at it.

Pages 144-145

This is one of my very favourite scenes. It was a last-minute decision to repeat the first panel of the scene in the last panel (it certainly wasn't in the script,) but I really like the way it adds to the sense of disappointment and futility the men experience when it appears that Charles has failed to find help. They are truly back where they started.

Plus, I always relish any opportunity to draw a birch bark canoe.

Pages 146-149

Another reason for stressing the moon in the previous scene was to, again, call attention to the different moon phase at the start of this one. The Charles story is, at this point, weeks ahead of the Fletcher story. Charles has been travelling for six weeks, but only a matter of days have passed at the fort. The two threads don't meet up again chronologically until the third act.

I worried that the antique spelling of "jail" on page 147 would throw people, but apparently it didn't. I should stop worrying and start giving the audience more credit.

After the wordy, expository nature of his last scene, it was nice to get back to the broodingly quiet Simon we met in act one by having him struggle silently with finding Kirby's note. My favourite Simon scenes to write and draw were these ones in which his loyalty is still on the fence.

Pages 151-156

Just as the prologue was a late decision, so too was this interlude. Initially, I had the second volume ending with the previous scene, and Fletcher nervously beginning to dig toward escape. It bothered me, though, that Eagle Eye—such an important character in the first volume—hadn't appeared in the second one. Given that he was scheduled to make a triumphant reappearance in the third, that was clearly too long for him to be absent from the story.

So one night while I was going to sleep (which is when all the best ideas come, shaking loose from a cluttered mind that's beginning to clear itself) this scene simply appeared, fully formed, as I scrambled to sketch it all out on my ever-present bedside notepad. That's the way it works—some ideas take a lot of tweaking and development to get them to work, others just show up pretty much ready for print. The panel where the Eagle reappears still gives me goose bumps, just like it did on the night it kept me from sleeping.

Pages 158-160

From the beginning, I thought of the two story threads as being each other's mirror image. One was about an old man who is hardened and experienced, the other about a young man who is naive and untested. One is about a rescue, the other about an escape. One protagonist wants to leave the fort, then is forced to fight his way back in. The other wants to come to the fort to prove himself, then is forced to fight his way back out. Charles is having to leave the New World, and is uncertain about it. Fletcher is coming to the New World, but isn't sure he wants to, either. And one story is about two fathers fighting over a son, while the other is about two sons fighting over a father.

So it was exciting to have these two rivals, Fletcher and Simon, alone and face-to-face at last. I wrote a *lot* here, but eventually pared it down to just three pages (it helped that some of the scene got moved to later in the chapter, and turned into a flashback.) I didn't want them spending too long talking to each other—it had to be clear that they didn't like each other, and that Fletcher was only trusting Simon out of necessity.

Pages 161-165

René de Cuthbert is a character that there needs to be some sympathy for later in the story, so treating his captivity from his point of view seemed like a natural way to get the ball rolling on that. I also liked the idea of revealing Charles and John Blackmoon together in this way at the beginning of volume three, as they're the last two things in the world you'd want to see if you were a French prisoner having their blindfold removed.

I bounced back and forth several times between René being French or his being Dutch or some other non-English European. I always *wanted* him to be French—mostly so I could have one French character who wasn't a villain—but I wasn't sure the audience would buy him changing sides and aiding the English in the end (although it happened all the time in history, especially among such non-military personnel.) I stuck with French, though, and apparently the audience was willing to go with me on it.

René is a character who, like John Blackmoon, is really only being introduced in this story and will have much more to do as the series progresses. By end of this story arc, he's the only Frenchman in a fort full of English, and that alone is worth pursuing.

Pages 166-169

I've stretched reality here to a degree, in that when a supply ship arrived in the Bay, it would normally have to turn right around and leave again, or risk being caught in ice in Hudson Strait—that's how short the sailing window was when taking the northern route into North America. There certainly wouldn't have been time to linger for weeks on end, as Montglave does, packing up and exerting psychological pressure on Simon.

I've left it somewhat vague as to what Montglave's motive really is—does he truly want Simon to come with him? Or does he simply, having failed to kill Charles, want to take away something precious to his old rival? I have my own thoughts on it, but this is the kind of thing that I think is best left up to the reader. I wrote it so that it would work either way, or both at once (in achieving the former, he would also certainly achieve the latter.)

Page 170

I had to keep cutting dialogue from this page, as it was all French and the translations ended up taking up so much space (panel four is still more crowded than I'd like.) But less writing is usually good. The leaner the dialogue, the better.

The hardest thing about writing the third act was deciding exactly when to reveal that Jack and his men were at the fort. I'd have preferred to hold onto that revelation until later, but it was necessary to get them there—and onto the supply ship—before the siege began. So, for the sake of practicality, this is where they landed.

Mostly, though, writing volume three was easy. I was completely in the groove, and all the pay-offs to all of the set-ups in volumes one and two came off as well or better than expected. I'd been working toward these scenes, and getting excited about them, for almost two years—now here I was writing them! The script came together in just two weeks, and was one of the most fun processes of the entire project.

Pages 171-172

Here Duncan voices what was a real issue in terms of defending HBC posts: it wasn't a military operation, as much as it may have seemed at times as formal and regulated as one. It was business, and as hardy as the occupants of the posts were, they were tradesmen, not warriors. Violent encounters such as the ones I've depicted did occur, but often the reluctant Bay men would simply surrender upon sight of enemy ships, rather than risk their lives for what was essentially just a paycheque.

Pages 173-177

I spent a long time trying to come up with the exact nature of Fletcher's escape plan. But I kept coming come back to the idea of him hiding in a barrel, for several reasons. First, it seemed fairly ingenious in its simplicity. Second, it was something that would require him to enlist Simon's help. Third, it was a nice tip of the hat to *The Hobbit*—if it worked for Tolkien, it works for me. Lastly, I liked the idea that he'd end up back in the ship's hold, exactly where he was first captured. A lot of things in the third volume echoed the first volume, so the symmetry of this particular situation was hard to resist.

Just don't ask me how Fletcher got the barrel's lid fastened after he got in it.

Pages 179-183

I joked with people that the third volume was "all killing and yelling." This scene is the start of both.

I thought it would be nice to have the French dialogue actually be in French, rather than having it appear translated via some sort of comic-book shorthand. It gives the French characters some flavour that they wouldn't have otherwise. However, despite having studied it in grades 7-10, my French is terrible, meaning I had to rely on translators to create French dialogue from my English script. Oni Press had someone they used for the first two volumes, but when they turned out at the last minute to be unavailable for the third, I was in a bit of a bind. Fortunately, my friend Diana Tamblyn (the Ignatz-nominated mini-comics artist) came to my quick rescue by introducing me to a professional translator named Lorraine Vincent. Lorraine did an excellent job, on very little notice, and didn't charge me a cent. Can't beat *that* with a stick.

Charles's plan to win back Fort Newcastle was loosely inspired by the brilliant 1697 siege of York Factory by Pierre Le Moyne d'Iberville (who would later found the colony of Louisiana.) The French naval captain and his small band of shipwrecked survivors forced the surrender of the HBC's North American headquarters by setting up snipers and pretending to be a much larger force. It remained in French hands until it was returned to England by the Treaty of Utrecht in 1713, the intervening years representing the longest stretch of time that any foreign power was able to quell the English fur trade monopoly in the Bay.

Pages 184-188

When it came time to write this scene, I was so happy that I'd given Fletcher this medical instrument back in chapter four. My original intention was that Fletcher would just sort of wake up with a start, causing the French to hear him, but when I remembered he had one of Kirby's surgical tools, it seemed natural to simply have it fall out of his hand, waking him and alerting the French both (and, of course, it also proved useful for stabbing people in the back with.) It's a lot more realistic, while also making Fletcher seem like less of a bumbling idiot. Sometimes you plan things in detail, sometimes happy accidents just occur.

"CHUK," by the way, is my favourite sound effect.

Pages 189-190

The relationship between Charles and René de Cuthbert was inspired by the relationship between Charlemagne and Ogier the Dane in Carolingian mythology. Ogier was a captive of Charlemagne's before proving himself—and earning his freedom—by saving the Frankish king's life on the battlefield. Much of *Northwest Passage* is inspired by the legends of Charlemagne, in fact, which I'm surprised nobody who's written about the series has picked up on—I even named the main character "Charles" in what I thought was an easily recognizable homage to his royal predecessor. I'd previously pitched Oni Press an historical fantasy series that would have tried to marry the mythological Charlemagne with his historical counterpart; they quickly passed. But I was able to spin a lot of the ideas from that pitch into a more novel setting, and *Northwest Passage* was born.

Pages 191-192

"Not appropriate for polite society" is a favourite expression of my good friend Chris Scholey, and I've given it to Jack here because he needed to say something witty and this just seemed to work. But it's also a tip of the hat to Chris, who was enormously helpful during the writing of this tale.

Though he's since moved on, Chris used to work for a prominent Toronto theatre company, and part of his job (among many other things) was working with writers to develop new plays. Early in my writing process for *Northwest Passage*, he graciously offered to take a look at my scripts, and I, still finding my feet as a writer, eagerly agreed to let him. When I arrived at a draft I was happy with for each volume, I sent it to Chris. He'd look over each, make copious notes, then we'd get together and he'd go through the script page-by-page, spending hours at a time making me defend myself on everything from the smallest nuances of dialogue to overarching questions of theme. He was both a test audience and well-meaning critic, and thanks to his input I was able to significantly fine-tune the final drafts. It really helped sharpen my thinking about the book knowing that I was going to have to get it by his keen reading skills and knack for story. Though the reader will never know it, his influence can be felt in virtually every scene.

Pages 193-198

I found a few resources for 18th century slang, and tried to pepper the dialogue with examples where it seemed appropriate. Duncan uses a lot of them: "grab yer flats and sharps," "blood and 'ounds," etc. I'm hoping that "cock and pie" is going to come back into popular usage, two and a half centuries later. I've been using it myself, around the house.

In the bottom left corner of page 198 you can see poor, unfortunate Reaney being shot and killed. He only barely appears in the third act, but I figured he was worthy of an "on-screen" (though tiny) death.

Pages 199-200

I wanted there to be at least one point during the climax of the story where the audience sees the entire fort at one time, to establish the geography of the battle that's about to take place. Viewing it from the deck of the supply ship seemed a natural choice. Drawing this panel took hours (in addition to the fort itself and the ship's rigging there was also a bunch of characters to deal with), as did inking it. But I think it does the job nicely.

Pages 201-206

This scene is my favourite in the entire story. It features my favourite character, Duncan, and the speech that he's been working up to for 200 pages. But I also consider it one of my best scenes in terms of sprucing up expository dialogue by concentrating on actions that tie into that dialogue metaphorically—in this case, Duncan using his knife to literally "pry" out the stoic Charles's feelings about Simon. The only reason I had Charles get shot was to create the opportunity for this tender yet highly charged and meaningful action between them. It's the high point for Duncan, yet the low point for Charles, and everything turns right here, punctuated by what happens next…

Page 207

I knew early on that because the supply ship was such a prominent part of the first act's capture of the fort, it was going to have to also be a prominent part of the third act's *re*capture of the fort. Having it simply float there throughout just felt wrong. And there was also the fact that I wanted Charles and the other survivors to be stranded at the end of the story, not simply able to

hop aboard the *Maid Marian* and sail away. So it was decided fairly quickly that the ship was going to have to explode, which also helped the plot along by creating the perfect diversion for Charles's second charge.

It should be noted, however, that my buddy Chris Scholey (whom I wrote about in the notes for pages 191-192) was against the idea, thinking that blowing something up was far too *Die Hard* for a piece of historical fiction. He was much more agreeable to the idea of Jack and his men firing on the fort with the ship's cannons (the dialogue on page 203 was written in response to this suggestion), then having the ship be sunk by Montglave's men firing from fort. I didn't think that was nearly *big* enough for such a turning point in the action, and figured Montglave wasn't dumb enough to sink the ship he was depending on to get home, so it became the one instance where I flat out ignored Chris's advice.

We still argue about it, occasionally. I've considered framing the original art of this page and giving it to him, just to be a bastard.

Pages 208-210

Though I outline each volume pretty thoroughly before writing, there are always surprises, this scene being a prime example. I really had no plans for Kirby beyond giving Fletcher the surgical tool and slipping Simon the note in act two. Those two critical actions were the reason I left him at the fort, allowing him to drop out of Charles's story and become part of Fletcher's. I knew he couldn't just disappear, though. Like the supply ship, he was present for the final battle and would therefore need to have some kind of role in it—I just had no idea what that role would be. I trusted that when he was needed, he would step forward—as he always does—and that's exactly what happened. I had no idea that Kirby would open the gate until I wrote the words (in my head, I just figured Charles and his men would enter the fort through one of the many holes that had been blown in the walls.) Careful planning is helpful, but if I learned anything from writing this story, it's to also stay open to these spontaneous moments when the characters begin to write themselves, surprising even the author who created them.

The original art for page 210 is owned by *Northwest Passage* editor Randal C. Jarrell, who offered to buy it after I sent in the pencils for this scene. Randy's enthusiasm for the project has always been enormous, which I'm thankful for. Like myself, he has a passion for history, and he's another person who makes the book better simply by my knowing it will need to pass his high standards.

Pages 211-212

Here, at last, the pay-off to Eagle Eye's story, which is one of the very earliest scenes I imagined, a bookend to the very opening of the story. It seems somewhat diminished on paper, but I'm not sure it ever could have been as a big a moment as it was in my head. I hope it's as satisfying to the reader as it was to me to see this jerk in the cocked hat finally get what's coming to him.

Many (mostly American) people who have written about the series have remarked that the relationship between the English and the Cree seems unrealistically friendly, but Canadian history is somewhat different than American history in that respect. Don't get me wrong, there were plenty of abuses of the Indians by the Europeans, many violent conflicts (particularly between the French and the Iroquois,) and we did, of course, end up claiming their land as our own. But given that Canada was largely settled by the fur trade, it was necessary to maintain, at minimum, a good business relationship with the Native people who provided the furs. Militarily, both England and France considered the Indians valuable trackers and warriors, and forged alliances with various tribes during their numerous colonial conflicts (the most notable being The Seven Years War.)

So it's not unrealistic that an HBC governor such as Charles might have befriended a prominent Cree like Eagle Eye. In fact, their relationship was largely inspired by the friendship between explorer Samuel Hearne (who later became the governor of Prince of Wales's Fort) and the Chipewyan chief Matonabbee. And besides, I hope it's obvious that these Cree warriors aren't so much rushing to the defence of the English as they are seeking revenge for the destruction of their village.

Pages 213-217

I initially wanted a longer fight sequence here where we'd follow various characters through the chaos of battle. I eventually cut it all down to just what appears on page 214, which I think does the trick of describing how the two groups are fighting their way toward each other, while also having the two storylines finally meeting up on the same page. Plus, the book was getting long. I'd figured volume three would be about the same length as volume one (67 story pages,) but it ended up being closer in length to volume two (88 story pages.) This chapter had more than enough fighting in it already, so I trimmed the excess for the sake of page count, and pace.

Another surprise: I had no idea that Duncan was going to be shot until I arrived at the top of page 215. All I knew as I began writing was that Charles would become distracted, creating the opportunity for René to save his life. So, I thought, what could happen that was big enough to make Charles lose his head during a fight? This was the only thing I could think of. Many fans I talked to were certain from reading the first volume that Duncan was going to die—that he just seemed too good, and too reluctantly drawn into Charles's struggle. That was never the plan, but I liked the idea of dangling the possibility in front of the audience here, however briefly (it should be clear from Duncan's appearance in the prologue that he's going to survive his wound, though I plan to make him suffer a long and uncomfortable recovery.)

Pages 218-219

It's interesting to note that in my original outline, Fletcher wasn't present for this final showdown at the governor's house. It was just Charles and Montglave, with Simon bouncing back and forth between them. It seems ridiculous now—after all, Fletcher's storyline is coming to its climax here too, by finally bringing him and Charles together in the same place. It goes back to what I wrote about Fletcher's story sometimes getting short shrift. Charles's story was mapped out in detail, while with Fletcher's I gave myself more room to discover the story as I wrote.

Pages 220-221

I had originally envisioned a lengthy and dramatic fight scene between these two characters, Charles's right-hand-man and Montglave's. But I eventually decided that I simply didn't want to put that trigger-happy weasel Zev anywhere near John Blackmoon's level. So I went in the complete opposite direction by having John dispose of Zev just as he did René's followers in chapter four—in the most quick and easy manner I could think of. He isn't even *armed.* I think it's a cool scene, makes a nice counterpoint to the more vigorous fighting going on below, and gives John Blackmoon a kick-ass "moment" during the big finale.

Pages 222-230

I really hoped that the "I am your father!" ending wouldn't strike people as being stereotypical. It's not a twist just for the sake of one…the entire story had been building to this revelation of the true source of tension between Charles and Simon.

Is Simon truly Montglave's son? I have no idea (I even designed Simon's appearance such that it would work either way, looking like both Charles and Montglave.) What's important is that Charles thought he was, and that he was never able to look at Simon without being reminded of his old enemy and the vicious rape of his wife. Simon, of course, interpreted Charles's coldness as being of some fault of his own, and resented him (and, eventually, all Whites) for it. Neither were able to talk about it, for fear of admitting their greatest fear to the other. So it too often goes with fathers and sons.

It's become something of recurring joke that *Northwest Passage* has only two female characters and that both appear only in flashback, as they're both dead. I worried that all the testosterone would alienate female readers, but it doesn't seem to have; I've gotten plenty of nice reviews and fan support from women. Bright Moon (and her father, Straight Arrow) will be making a return to the pages of this series soon, in a prominent role, so it's not going to be just a boy's club.

I call panel two on page 229 "my Frank Miller shot." I always liked the way Miller occasionally used the sound effect as the panel border, as if nothing else exists but the sound of the gun.

I liked the idea of Charles, after the shooting, repeating his dialogue from the breakfast scene way back at the beginning of chapter two. All the cards are now on the table, but they still can't talk about them. They're right back where they started. For me, one of the most attractive things about the story was that Charles would succeed at recapturing the fort, but fail at this. Until you turn to that final page—"I am not your son"—you think that Charles has come out on top. But he hasn't. He's lost.

Pages 232-235

I thought it was important for the epilogue, right off the top, to show who was still alive at the fort. Not very many people, as it turns out. It's really just the "name" characters at this point, and two or three others. Much of the rest of the series, as it unfolds, will deal with the attempts of this small band to simply stay alive.

It was a last minute decision to have Charles light a pipe before going inside. It wasn't in the script. But it felt like a natural thing for him to do, given the context of the scene. It was quite accidental that I happened to give one to Hargrove during his scene with Fletcher in act one—Fletcher is a character in search of a father figure, and smoking a pipe just seemed like a "fatherly" thing for Hargrove to be doing in that scene as he schooled the younger man in the ways of the New World. It occurred to me that I could do the same in act two, during one of the Montglave/Simon scenes, as a way of suggesting that Montglave was becoming "father" to Simon (perhaps literally, as we find out at the story's climax.) So what else would I have had Charles do here, the final of the book's father figures, as he prepares to once more and forever forgo his own ambitions and accept the responsibility of leadership?

As I've written previously, sometimes you plan these sorts of connections meticulously, other times you only recognize them when they appear. Whatever muse sends them, I'm thankful. It wouldn't have been the same ending, I don't think, without Charles lighting that pipe.

— Scott Chantler

December 2006

The Annotated

NORTHWEST PASSAGE

Original Cover Gallery

NORTHWEST
PASSAGE
PULSE-POUNDING WESTERN ACTION
by SCOTT CHANTLER
2

NORTHWEST
PASSAGE
BARE-KNUCKLED FRONTIER COMBAT
by SCOTT CHANTLER
3

Other Books From Oni Press...

DAYS LIKE THIS™
written by J. Torres;
illustrated by Scott Chantler
88 pages, $8.95 US
ISBN 978-1-929998-48-7

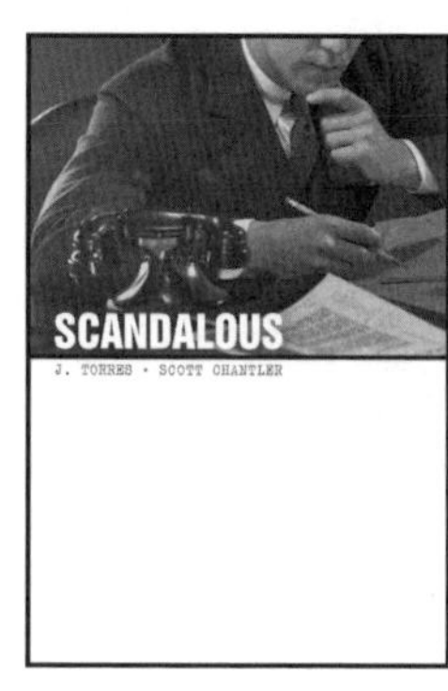

SCANDALOUS™
written by J. Torres;
illustrated by Scott Chantler
104 pages, $9.95 US
ISBN 978-1929998-98-2

CAPOTE IN KANSAS™
written by Ande Parks;
illustrated by Chris Samnee
128 pages, $11.95 US
ISBN: 978-1-932664-29-4

THE LONG HAUL™
written by Antony Johnston;
illustrated by Eduardo Barreto
176 pages, $14.95 US
ISBN 978-1-932664-05-8

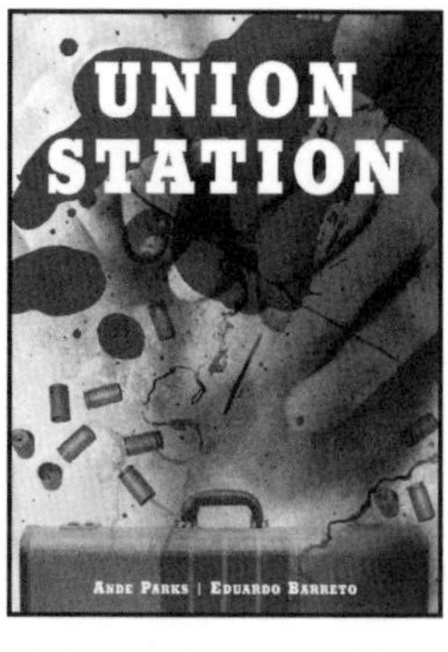

UNION STATION™
written by Ande Parks;
illustrated by Eduardo Barreto
128 pages, $11.95 US
ISBN 978-1929998-69-2

POLLY AND THE PIRATES™
written and illustrated
by Ted Naifeh
176 pages, $11.95 US
ISBN: 978-1-932664-46-1

Available at finer comics shops everywhere. For a comics store near you, call 1-888-COMIC-BOOK or visit www.the-master-list.com. For more Oni Press titles and information visit www.onipress.com.